Football for Young Champions

ROBERT J. ANTONACCI
and
JENE BARR

Illustrated by RUS ANDERSON

FOOTBALL
for
YOUNG CHAMPIONS

McGraw-Hill Book Company
New York   Toronto   London   Sydney
St. Louis   San Francisco
Mexico   Panama

Also by Robert J. Antonacci and Jene Barr

BASEBALL FOR YOUNG CHAMPIONS
BASKETBALL FOR YOUNG CHAMPIONS
PHYSICAL FITNESS FOR YOUNG CHAMPIONS

Robert J. Antonacci is a coauthor of

SPORTS OFFICIATING

Jene Barr is author of

BIG WHEELS! LITTLE WHEELS!

TEXAS PETE, LITTLE COWBOY

MIKE THE MILKMAN

and others

796.33

c. 1

CONTENTS

CHAPTER 1

FOOTBALL: THE GREAT FIELD GAME

The "Kickoff!"

"Ready!"

The umpire raises his hand for the kickoff. Both teams are lined up, ready to go. It's the sturdy Beavers against the husky Badgers.

Listen! The referee blows his whistle. In the stands the crowd leans forward. The game is on!

The Badger kickoff man runs toward the ball. With a strong kick the ball sails through the air. At the other end of the field stands the Beaver player, Speedy Pete, the long-runner.

With the speed of light, he runs toward the ball. It

7

lands squarely in his arms. Hugging the ball, Pete streaks toward the goal.

He's on the 40-yard line! The 30! The 20! The crowd is on its feet. The cheerleaders jump up and down. In the stands, a man in a heavy fur coat loses his cap. A girl breaks her team flag. Just ahead looms the goal.

With a mighty spurt, Pete dashes across the line. It's a touchdown! Speedy Pete, the long-runner, has done it again!

This is American football! But, how different it is from the game that was played long ago.

Football in Other Lands

"Kicking the Skull!" In ancient times, young Greek and Roman boys played a simple kicking game. Many years later, in England, some young men who worked in the fields dug up some skulls. They kicked these skulls along the ground and this became a game.

A group of boys would try to kick a skull past another group. This game was called "Kicking the Skull." But the skulls were hard and hurt the feet. So the boys stuffed animal bladders and kicked them. Great numbers of players took part in this game. They would kick the bladder from one town into the next. What a dangerous game these young men played!

To make the game safer. each team marked a definite

goal line and decided upon a certain number of players. This game developed into soccer. The name "soccer" came about because the game was originally called "Association football," which in turn became known as "Association," "Soc," "Socker," and finally, "Soccer."

Soccer. In soccer, except in one or two special cases, a player must never use his hands or run with the ball. The ball may be kicked, or a player may use his head, elbow, or chest to bounce or move the ball along.

Rugby Football. During a soccer game played at the Rugby School in England in 1823, one of the players made a mistake. He picked up the ball and *ran* with it toward the goal for a touchdown. It was exciting! In time, other schools allowed their players to run with the ball. This game was named "Rugby's football," which became "Rugby football" and in time "Rugby."

Football in America

During the Colonial days in America, boys played a kicking game which was very much like soccer. They used a round ball. There were no fixed rules or any set number of players.

First Football Games. In 1869 Princeton played against Rutgers. This was the first game played by two American colleges in the United States. But it was not regular football because it was played under soccer rules.

The first football game played by an American team against a team from another country took place in 1873 between Harvard University and the Eton School of England. A combination of Rugby and soccer was played. For the first time, eleven men were used on a team. And eleven men are used today!

First Football Association. When the Eastern colleges organized the Intercollegiate Football Association, they still played the soccer brand of football, which was mostly kicking. Then later in 1876, the Association adopted two very important rules:

    1. There shall be eleven men on a team.

    2. Players may run with the ball.

With the addition of these rules, American football was on its way!

Playing Positions Are Named. Teams now lined up their players on the field in a certain order. The team with the ball placed seven men in a line. These were the "scrimmage-line" players and were named "linemen."

Behind the scrimmage line stood the "ball-carriers." They were named "backfield players." The backfield player who called the plays was named the "quarter-back."

First Use of Signals. As the game took shape, teams

began to use signals. These signals told which play to use and when the center should "snap" the ball to a backfield player.

At first, the signals were whole sentences. Then the letters of the alphabet were used. Nowadays the quarterback uses numbers.

Downs. Years ago a team was allowed three downs in which to advance the ball a distance of 5 yards. In 1906 this rule was changed. A team had to advance a distance of 10 yards within four downs in order to keep the ball. This rule is still used today.

Cheering at Games. Shortly after the Civil War, the players would run out on the field before a game and give a few loud cheers for themselves. Probably they did this to build up their own confidence. They also hoped these yells would frighten the opposing team. (They probably frightened the fans, too.)

The "Big Ten." As football became more popular, colleges in each part of the country formed leagues, or conferences. These conferences arranged playing schedules for their schools. They chose the champion team at the end of the season also.

The Middle West organized the first league, the Western Conference, in 1896. This league, known as the "Big Ten," is still going strong.

Some teams, such as Notre Dame, Army, and Navy, do not belong to any conference. They arrange their own schedules and play any team they wish.

FOOTBALL ARMOR 1902

REFEREE

EARLY AMERICAN FOOTBALL GAME 1890's

Football Almost Disappears! Years ago football was a rough game and many players were hurt. Then something happened which changed the whole future of the game.

A certain team wanted to make sure they would win a coming game. They decided to play rough against the star player of the opposing team. This player was badly hurt. Everyone was shocked at such poor sportsmanship. Theodore Roosevelt, then President of the United States, threatened to end the game of football if rough playing did not stop.

Very quickly the colleges worked out safer playing rules. New skills were put into use. Players learned that strength alone could not win a game. And these new skills saved the game of football.

First Forward Pass. One of the new skills was very exciting. A man could throw the ball over the heads of the enemy players and into the arms of a teammate for a long gain. This play was called the "forward pass." The forward pass became a game rule for the first time in 1906.

Who threw the first forward pass? To this very day football fans argue over this point. It makes good football talk.

A Big Upset. In 1913 West Point had one of the best teams in the country. They needed one more game to complete their schedule for that season. West

Point decided to ask Notre Dame to play against them.

Everyone felt sorry for Notre Dame because they were a little team. They were not known. All the football fans were sure that the Army team would beat them badly.

The game started. Notre Dame began to throw passes for long gains and touchdowns. The fans couldn't believe their eyes. The rest is now football history. West Point lost.

After this game, schools wanted coaches who could teach the forward pass. Football was now a much faster game. Action took place over the whole field. The players had to think fast and move fast.

First Uniforms. In the early days a player was considered a "softie" if he wore any kind of protective clothing. No one wore a helmet to protect his head. Instead, players let their hair grow thick before a game.

Princeton was the first to upset this childish idea. They began wearing tight canvas jackets which laced up in the front. Then a rule was passed stating that all players must wear protective clothing.

First Footballs. The first footballs were round because the early games were really soccer football. After Rugby football came into style, the ball became more egg-shaped. About 1897 the ball began to look more like the football of today.

Players Get Numbers. In 1915 the University of Pittsburgh put numbers on the jerseys of their players.

Nowadays each player must wear a number on the front and back of his jersey. These numbers help tell who the players are and what they are doing.

First Professional Teams. Pittsburgh was the first big city to have a professional team. To make professional football more popular, the National Football League was formed. This league is now divided into two groups, the Eastern and Western Divisions.

First "All-American." Walter Camp has been called the "Father of American Football." As a young man he was an outstanding player at Yale.

In 1889 he began to choose the best college players from all over the country as "All-American" players. Nowadays there are many All-American lists. The dream of every college player is to be chosen as an All-American.

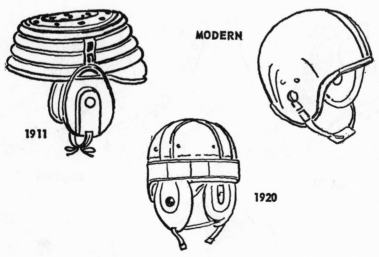

1911

MODERN

1920

National Football Hall of Fame. Plans are being made for a Football Hall of Fame. It will be located on the grounds of Rutgers University in New Brunswick, New Jersey. This place was chosen because the first college football game in America, played between Rutgers and Princeton, took place there in 1869.

Early uniforms, equipment, trophies, and important playing records will be on display. This memorial will honor the men who have tried to teach good sportsmanship through the game of football, and have helped young men become good citizens.

"Bowl Games." The idea of the bowl game is to have a deciding game between the two top college teams after the regular football season is over.

The Rose Bowl Game is played on New Year's Day in Pasadena, California. Other cities also sponsor

FOOTBALL SHOES

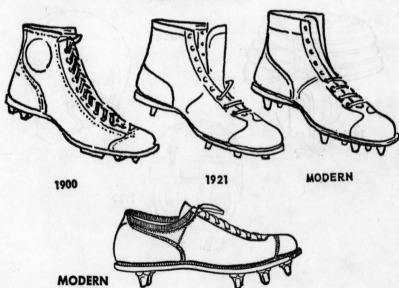

1900   1921   MODERN

MODERN

bowl games. Miami, Florida, has the Orange Bowl. New Orleans, Louisiana, is known for its Sugar Bowl. Dallas, Texas, is famous for the Cotton Bowl. And there are many others.

More Championship Games. In addition to bowl, college, and professional championships for the grown-ups, there are school and neighborhood championships for younger players. There are also touch football championships open to young players in neighborhood leagues, schools, and playgrounds. Many champion players started by playing touch football with these community leagues.

Touch Football, an American Game. Football is enjoyed all over the world. But in the United States,

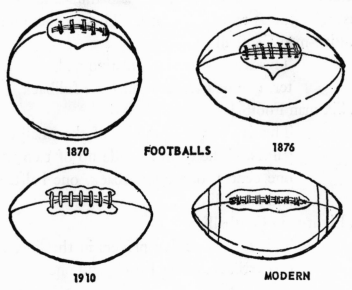

1870   **FOOTBALLS**   1876

1910   **MODERN**

some form of touch football is played on almost every playground in the land. Schools play this game. So do office and factory workers. Fathers and sons like to practice this game together.

Because this game is played by more people than all other football games combined, touch football may well be called an "American" game.

Other Football Games. There are small schools and colleges that do not have enough students for regular eleven-man football teams. Some cannot afford to buy so many uniforms. To make it possible for these schools to enjoy the game, other forms of football have been invented.

These games use fewer players, a smaller playing field, and shorter playing time. But the game itself is just the same as regular football. These games are:

1. Five-man Football

    This team is made up of two ends, one center, one quarterback, and one fullback.

2. Six-man Football

    This is the most popular of the small-team games. The team is made up of two ends, one center, one quarterback, one halfback, and one fullback.

3. Eight-man Football

    This team uses five players in the line, one quarterback, one halfback, and one fullback.

CHAPTER 2

KNOW YOUR FOOTBALL

Go to football games. Watch them over TV or listen to games on the radio. Read the newspapers, magazines, and books. As you listen, watch, and read, you will see that football is a battle of brains and skill.

One team are the attackers. They have possession of the ball. The opposing team are the defenders and they try to defend their goal. The attackers move into the defenders' territory. They hammer their way through the defenders' line. They want to score a touchdown. But wait! The defending team fights back. They try to capture the ball. This is football!

To enjoy a game it is necessary to understand it. After you get to know football, no doubt you will qualify as a "Monday-morning quarterback" and will be able to tell people how you would have played the game.

Before the Game

Is your favorite team going to play? Who are the players? What are their playing records? What is the record of their team?

Read the newspapers and learn the numbers of the players, their positions, and their ages and weights. Sports writers give much information about players and teams.

The Playing Field

The actual playing field is 300 feet long and 160 feet wide. On each end of the field stand the goal posts.

The Players

There are eleven players on a regular football team. Every player has a definite position. The positions are:

four backfield players which consist of—
> one quarterback
> one left halfback
> one right halfback
> one fullback

seven line players—
> one left end
> one left tackle
> one left guard
> one center

one right guard
one right tackle
one right end

Length of Game

Most regular football games last sixty minutes of actual playing time. The game is divided into four periods called "quarters." Each quarter lasts fifteen minutes. After the second quarter, the teams get fifteen minutes of rest off the field. High school games have four 12-minute quarters.

Warm-up Practice

Before a game the players have warm-up practice. The whole team, even the substitutes, are out on the field. The backfield men throw passes. The ends practice catching passes. All the centers drill on "snapping" the ball to the backfield players. The linemen practice tackling and blocking.

Getting Ready for the Kickoff

The referee calls the team captains to the center of the field to decide which team will kick off. The referee tosses a coin into the air. The winner of the toss may choose to have the kickoff or receive the ball. The loser chooses which goal he wishes to defend.

The Kickoff!

Both teams line up on the field. The referee places the ball on the 40-yard line. He raises his hand and blows his whistle as the signal to start the game. The game is on!

The team that has the ball makes the kickoff. The kicker runs toward the ball, and with a strong kick sends it sailing to the other end of the field.

"First Down—10 Yards to Go!"

When the fans hear this, they know that the team with the ball is "on the move." The "down" is the very heart of football. Through the system of making downs, a team can hammer its way across the field to their opponent's goal for a touchdown. What is a down?

A "down" is a *play* which begins when the center "snaps" the ball back to a player. A team is given a set of four downs in which to advance the ball 10 yards closer to the goal. At the end of each down the ball is dead. Then another down begins. If a team succeeds in making their 10 yards (or more) within the four downs, it is called a "first down," and they receive another set of four downs.

A team keeps possession of the ball as long as they continue to make their sets of four downs or make a score. But if they do not make their 10 yards, they give up the ball to the other team.

The Huddle and Signals

Before every play the team with the ball goes into a "huddle." The huddle forms about 10 yards behind the spot where the ball is on the ground.

In the huddle, the quarterback tells the signal for the next play. Then the players break the huddle and line up on the field in the formation they will use.

The Scrimmage Line

All through football one hears the term, "scrimmage line." The team with the ball lines up even with, or just behind, the ball which is on the ground. These line players form what is called the "scrimmage line." A scrimmage line may form anywhere on the field.

The team that does not have the ball must line up a yard away from the ball, facing their opponents. This space between the two teams is called the "scrimmage area" or "neutral zone."

Points in Scoring

In football there are four ways in which a team may score.

1. A touchdown, which counts for six points.

2. A try for an extra-point-after touchdown by making:
   a. a place kick over the cross bar and between the goal posts.
   b. a completed pass over the goal line.
      This gives one point for high school teams and two points for college teams.
   c. a run over the goal line.
      This gives one point for high school teams and two points for college teams.
3. A field goal, which earns three points.
4. A safety, which counts for two points.

The Touchdown

It's a thrill to see a man carry the ball across the line for a touchdown. In every game the touchdown is an exciting play. A touchdown can be made:
1. By running the ball across the goal line.
2. By catching a pass over the goal line.
3. When a team without the ball recovers an opponent's fumble behind the goal line.

Field-Goal Score

When a team feels that they cannot score or even make a first down, they may try a field-goal kick. This play is very much like the "kick-after-touchdown."

24

Scoring a Safety

A "safety" can be made only in back of the goal line. When a player receives the ball from one of his teammates and is tackled behind his own goal line by an enemy player this play is called a "safety." It scores two points for the team that made the tackle. The team that has been scored against must now kick off from their own 20-yard line.

Touchback

A "touchback" is often confused with a safety. It is a touchback:

1. When a punt or pass is caught by an opponent behind his own goal line and he does not try to run it back.
2. When a punted ball crosses the goal line and is not caught. The team that has kicked or passed, loses the ball.

There is no score for a touchback. The defending team takes possession of the ball. It is placed on their 20-yard line and put into play by them from a "center-snapback."

Passing

It's a thrill to watch a long pass sail down a football field. There are "forward" and "lateral" passes. The forward pass is one of the most popular plays.

Forward Pass. The forward pass is thrown forward to an eligible teammate in the direction of the opponents' goal. This pass may be thrown only from behind the line of scrimmage.

Lateral Pass. In making a lateral pass, the passer must throw the ball toward his side or to the rear. This pass may be thrown at any time and from any place on the field.

Completed Pass. When a forward pass is caught by an eligible player on the passer's own team, it is considered a "completed" pass.

Incompleted Pass. If a ball touches the ground before being caught by the player to whom it was thrown, it is an "incompleted" pass.

Intercepted Pass. When a player throws a pass to one of his teammates and it is caught by an enemy player, it is an "intercepted" pass.

Rules and Penalties

Coaches and teachers drill their teams to make sure they know and understand the rules of the game. Football fans should know the rules, too.

Penalties. If a team breaks one or more rules, it must pay a penalty. At the moment an official sees a rule broken, he blows his whistle and picks up the ball. With his hands he gives signs which tell:

      a. what the penalty is for
      b. against which team it was called
      c. against which player it was called
      d. what the penalty will be

"Off-side" Penalty. When a player charges forward and crosses the scrimmage line before the center snaps the ball, his team receives an off-side penalty. This penalty may be given either team.

Pass "Interference." When a player reaches to catch a pass from one of his teammates, and a man from the opposing team pushes or blocks him, it is a pass interference. This is considered a "completed" pass and an automatic "first down" for the team in possession of the ball.

"Rough-Play" Penalties. No player may hold, trip, kick, or knee anyone on the field. These tactics are considered "rough play" and may cost a team up to 15 yards in penalties.

"Clipping." When a player blocks another player from the rear, it is called "clipping." A fifteen-yard penalty is charged for this rough play.

"Out of Bounds." A ball is "out of bounds" when, for any reason, it goes out of the playing area of the field.

When a ball is "out of bounds" it is called a "dead ball." A dead ball must be put back into play by the officials.

Substitutions. In school and college football there is a strict "substitution" rule that tells when and how often substitutes may enter a game.

Professional teams have a "free substitution" rule which allows players to enter or leave a game at any time. Knowing all these rules makes it easier and more enjoyable to follow the game.

CHAPTER 3

FOOTBALL FORMATIONS

After every huddle a team lines up on the field ready for a certain play. The way the team lines up is called a "formation."

Different formations are used for offensive and defensive plays. A team is on the offensive when they have possession of the ball. They are on the defensive when they do not have the ball. There are many formations and a wise coach chooses the right one for each play.

Offensive Formations

T-Formation. One of the most popular is called "T-formation." When an even number of players stand on each side of the center, it is called a "balanced T." When there are more players on one side than the other, it is an unbalanced line.

T-Formation with a Balanced Line. The T-formation calls for speedy plays, quick blocking, and clever faking.

1. Three players stand on each side of the center and form the line.
2. The quarterback stands directly behind the center, ready to receive the ball.
3. The halfbacks stand about 3 yards behind the tackles.
4. The fullback stands about 4 yards behind the quarterback.

"Split" T-Formation. The "split-T" gets its name because the linemen "split" or stand farther apart on the line of scrimmage. This forces the enemy players to spread out also. In this way, the ball-carriers have a better chance to run through the enemy line.

"Winged" T-Formation. A "wing" can be formed on the right or left side of the line. In the winged-T, one of the halfbacks moves outward and forward toward the end player and forms a "wing." The player who makes the wing is called a "wingback." This formation adds strength or power on the side where the wing is formed.

Single Wing. The "single wing" can also form to the right or left side and is usually an unbalanced line.

Single Wing: Unbalanced Line to the Right. As

most of the players are on the right side, that part of the field has great strength for the coming play.

1. The center gets over the ball.
2. Two linemen take their places on his left side.
3. Four linemen take their positions on his right side. Watch the backfield players form the single wing.
   a. The right halfback, called the "wingback," moves up about a yard behind the right end.
   b. The quarterback stands about a yard away from the right halfback.
   c. The fullback stands 3 yards in back of the line and about 1½ yards away from the quarterback.
   d. The left halfback stands about 4 yards directly behind the center and 2 yards away from the fullback. He forms the tail of the wing and is called the "tailback."

Double Wing. The "double wing" can form as a balanced or unbalanced line.

Double Wing: Unbalanced Line to the Right. This is a good formation for passing and reverse running plays.

1. The linemen take their places on each side of the center, two on his left and four on his right side.
2. A wingback stands about a yard behind each end.
3. The fullback is 3 yards behind the right guard.
4. The tailback stands 5 yards behind the center.

OFFENSIVE FORMATIONS

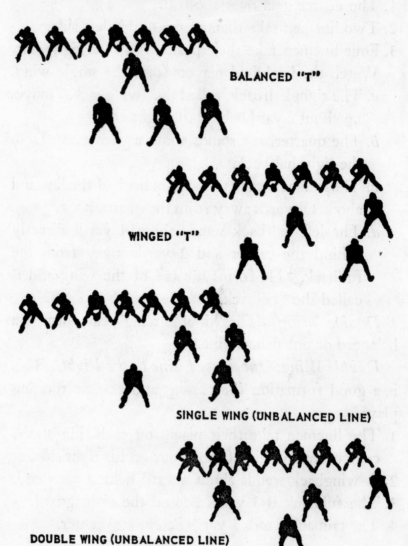

BALANCED "T"

WINGED "T"

SINGLE WING (UNBALANCED LINE)

DOUBLE WING (UNBALANCED LINE)

SHORT PUNT (BALANCED)

LONG PUNT FORMATION

SPLIT "T"

Long-punt Formation

1. Three linemen take their places on each side of the center.
2. The punter stands from 7 to 10 yards behind the center.
3. Two backfield players, about a yard apart, line up behind the right tackle.
4. The other backfield player stands behind the left tackle.

Short-punt Formation. This formation is almost the same as for the "long punt," but the punter (or tailback) does not stand as far back on the field.

The tailback is in a good position to make a quick kick, pass, or run. This formation is a good one for "reverses" and "plunges" into the line. Study and practice these formations one at a time. The correct formation for each play helps win games.

Defensive Formations

A team that does not have the ball must choose a formation that will stop the other team from gaining ground.

6-2-2-1 Defense. This defense is used against a team lined up in a balanced T-formation.

a. Six men stand on the line of scrimmage.
b. Two men stand in the second line and are called "linebackers."

"6-2-2-1"

"7-2-2"

"7-1-2-1"

DEFENSIVE FORMATIONS

c. Two players stand in the third line.

d. Farthest back on the field stands the "safety man."

7-2-2 *Defense.* This formation shows a strong, solid front-line defense. It is often used against short passes and running attacks.

a. Seven players defend on the line of scrimmage.

b. In the second line, one man stands behind each tackle.

c. In the third line, one player stands behind each end.

7-1-2-1 *Defense.* This defense is used to stop a team from making wide end runs.

a. Seven men are in the line of scrimmage.

b. In the next line, one man stands between the center and guard.

c. In the third line, one man stands directly behind each end.

d. Farthest back, directly in line with the center, stands the safety man.

Pass Defenses

1. Man-for-man Defense

Each defensive backfield player must guard a certain enemy end or backfield man. The defense backfield players must try to knock down or intercept passes thrown to the players they are guarding.

2. Zone Pass Defense

Each backfield player guards a certain area. He must prevent enemy players from catching passes in the area he is guarding.

Make up your own football formations and try them out. Study and practice the defense plays. This extra drill work is what makes champion players.

CHAPTER 4

HOW TO PASS

All youngsters like to throw a football. Don't you? It's exciting to throw a perfect pass that's caught by a running teammate.

Learning to Pass

At first, practice with a smaller-sized ball. Throw short, simple passes. Learn to control the ball. Then try to improve your aim.

A good pair of hands is needed for passing, but don't be discouraged if you are small and do not have big hands. Many fine players have small hands and are not big men.

Pass-receivers

When a team has the ball, passes may be caught only by the two ends and the four backfield players. These players are called "pass-receivers."

RUNNING PASS

JUMP PASS   RUNNING BACK TO PASS

When a team does not have the ball, any player may catch or "intercept" a pass.

The Different Passes

At a big game many kinds of passes are used. Most often you will see:

Forward Passes
1. Stationary pass
2. Short, and long, running passes
3. Jump pass
4. Fake pass

Lateral Passes
1. "Basketball-push" pass
2. Underhand "pitch-out" pass

Practice the forward stationary and short, running

GRIP FOR FORWARD PASS

READY FOR THROW

passes. Then try the lateral basketball-push pass and underhand pitch-out pass. A good player mixes his passes to keep the other team guessing.

Forward-pass Grip

The "grip" for all forward passes is the same. Left-handers will use the opposite hand and foot all the way through.

1. With both hands, hold the ball in front of you about level with your chin.
2. Spread the fingers of your right hand over the laces. Wrap your thumb around and underneath the ball. Hold the ball slightly behind the middle part.
3. Steady the ball with your left hand and bring it close to your right ear.

THE THROW

FOLLOW-THROUGH

4. Make a quarter-turn toward the right so that your left foot is facing toward your target. The target is the person to whom you are aiming the ball.

The Throw

1. Lean back just a little. Bend the right (back) knee a trifle and put your weight on the right foot.
2. At the same time, start to raise the left (front) foot.
3. Quickly take the left (front) hand away from the ball.
4. Take a short step forward toward the target with the left foot.
5. Push forward with the right foot, keeping the front end of the ball pointed a bit upward and your elbow pointed downward.
6. Throw the ball forward with a nice "whip" to give it a "spiral" twist. To get that spiral twist, release the ball from your fingertips.

The "Follow-through"

After the throw, shift your weight to the left (front) foot. Follow through with your throwing arm pointing toward the target. Do not grip the ball too tightly. Work for a smooth follow-through.

Stationary Pass. After you receive the ball, take your passing position. Aim for your target and make the throw.

Running Pass. Begin running with the ball. Then throw a pass while "on the run."

Jump Pass. Start running. At the right moment, jump up and throw a pass over your opponent's head.

"Fake" Passes. Pretend to throw a pass to a teammate. Instead, throw the pass to another player or run with the ball yourself.

Lateral Passes

Only the champion players use all the lateral pass grips. At this time, the two grips you will use most are the "Basketball-lateral" Grip and the "Underhand-lateral-pass" Grip. All lateral passes must be thrown *only* toward the side or rear, never forward.

"Basketball-lateral-push" Pass

1. Hold the ball around its middle with both hands, about waist-high.
2. Turn toward the player who will make the catch and bring the ball up to your chest.
3. As in basketball, push the ball to your teammate who is at your side or behind you. That's all there is to it.

Underhand "Pitch-out" Pass

1. Place both hands somewhat under the ball, with

your thumbs at the top and your fingers around the bottom.

2. Make a quick quarter-turn toward the right (or left) and hug the ball about waist-high.

3. With an underhand toss, throw the ball to your teammate.

These two passes may be made from a standing or running position. Practice until your timing is right.

PASSING HINTS

Hold the ball firmly behind the middle point. Never squeeze it.

The front end of the ball should point a bit upward. Never point the ball toward the ground.

Always point the front foot toward the target. Put your body behind the throw.

UNDERHAND-LATERAL-PASS

44

Do not practice football in the house!

A house is not the place for football.

Also, your mother wouldn't like it.

Forward-pass Drills. *For one player.*

1. Hold the ball with both hands. Twirl it between your hands. Stop the twirl. Take the "forward-pass" grip and pretend to make a pass.
2. Place the ball on the ground. Quickly pick it up, take the forward-pass grip and go through the motion of the throw.
3. Hang an old tire on a tree or from the cross-bar of a goal post. If it's a tree, be sure that it is not near anyone's house.

   Stand a short distance away and try throwing the ball through the tire. Then move back and increase your throwing distance. When you can do this well, start the tire swinging from side to side and try to pass the ball through this swinging target. Fun, isn't it?

Partner Drills

1. Face your partner at a distance of 5 yards. Throw passes to one another about chest-high. Keep moving back to increase the distance. Practice until you can make long, clean passes.

2. *For two or more players.*

One player acts as a center. The passer stands about 4 yards behind him. The center snaps the ball back to the passer, then runs forward a short distance to catch the pass that is being thrown.

If there are more than two players, line up behind one another at one side of the center. One at a time, each player runs out to catch a pass.

Lateral-pass Drills

1. Hold the ball in both hands. Bend the knees a little and stand with both feet about 12 inches apart. Your partner will stand about a yard away to your right. At the word "Go!" make a quick quarter-turn to the right, while your partner starts a slow run toward his right. Run after your partner as though you were chasing him. Then throw an easy two-handed "basketball" or "underhand" pass to him.

2. Do this same drill, but have a center snap the ball back to you.

CHAPTER 5

HOW TO KICK AND PUNT

You will remember that football started as a "kicking" game. Although the game has changed a great deal, kicking is still very important. Every player should know how to kick and "punt." What are the different kicks? When are they used? How are they made?

Football Kicks

1. The Punt
2. Kickoff
3. Place kick
4. Field goal

What a Punter Must Know. A successful punt can turn defeat into victory. The punt is used when other plays won't work, or when a team is in trouble. To become a good punter, you must know how to:

1. Take the punter's "stance."
2. Hold the ball before the punt.
3. Take the steps before the punt.
4. Drop the ball on the "kicking" foot.
5. Balance on one foot while the other foot is about to make the punt.
6. Follow through on the kick.

Write this information in your Football Notebook.

"Stance" for Making the Punt

1. Stand relaxed, with your kicking foot a little ahead of your other foot.
2. Lean your body a bit forward and bend your knees.
3. Stretch your arms about knee-high, with your fingers spread and fingertips pointed a trifle downward. You are ready to receive the ball.

Receiving Ball for the Punt. Keep your eyes on the ball as the center snaps it right into your hands. Shift

WAITING TO RECEIVE BALL

THE PUNT

48

the ball into position so that it is level (parallel) with the ground. Place the opposite hand to your kicking foot toward the front of the ball, and your other hand toward the rear of the ball. If the ball has laces turn it so that the laces face upward.

Steps for the Punt

1. Hold the ball about waist-high and take a quick, short step with your (forward) kicking foot.
2. Take a regular-sized step with your other foot and turn the front end of the ball slightly in the same direction.
3. Your kicking foot is behind you, ready to make the kick.

The Punt

1. Keep the knee of your kicking foot slightly bent.

THE PUNT

2. As your kicking leg begins to move forward, lower the ball and release it just above knee-height with your front hand. Then quickly remove your other hand.
3. Point the toes of your kicking foot forward and a bit inward, keeping your ankle rigid. All your weight should be on the other foot.
4. Now comes the kick! With a nice "whipping" action, your kicking foot meets the ball at the instep at about knee-height.

Punt "Follow-through." After the kick, straighten your knee and continue the kicking motion. This "follow-through" will give the ball extra distance and height as it sails down the field.

Practice the stance, steps for the punt, kick, and follow-through, in slow motion until you can do them smoothly.

"Spiral" Punting. To make the ball "spiral," move the front end of the ball slightly in the opposite direction from your kicking foot. Then drop the ball lightly upon the instep of your kicking foot and let go with the kick. That's all there is to it. Make sure that the instep meets the ball at the proper angle.

PUNTING HINTS

Punt with your instep. Never with your toes.

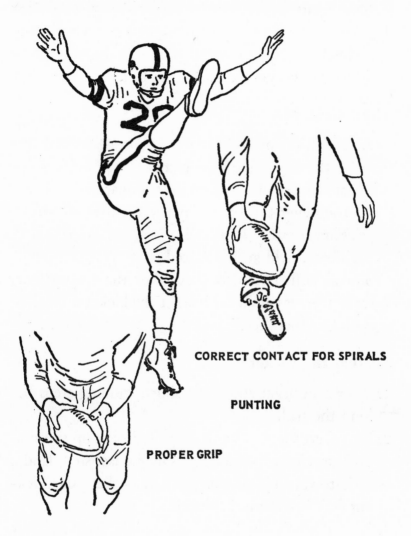

CORRECT CONTACT FOR SPIRALS

PUNTING

PROPER GRIP

Swing your leg forward with the toe pointed inward during the kick.

Keep your weight on the toes of your supporting foot. Never jump off the ground when making a punt.

Always keep your eyes on the ball.

The "Kickoff"

A team kicks off—
   a. at the beginning of a game
   b. at the beginning of the third quarter
   c. following the extra play after a touchdown
   d. after a safety is scored
   e. after a field goal is scored

The kickoff starts with the ball on the 40-yard line. A teammate may hold the ball, or the kicker may place it upon a rubber "tee."

Making the Kickoff

1. Take a position about ten short, running steps behind the ball.
2. Run with short, smooth steps and pick up speed as you get closer to the ball. On the last step, land a little toward the side of the ball so that your kicking foot is directly behind it.
3. Kick the ball just below the middle, keeping your knee and ankle stiff.

KICKOFF

4. After the kick, keep running toward the player who is making the catch.

Practice your "timing" by learning how many steps to take before making the kick. Not all players use the same number of steps.

"Place Kick" for Point-after-touchdown.

The "place kick" is tried only after a touchdown. In this play, the object is to kick the ball between the goal posts and over the cross-bar.

The ball is placed on the ground at the 2-yard line, in front of the goal posts where the center will snap it back. Mark a spot on the ground where the "ball-holder" will hold the ball for the kicker.

The ball-holder takes a position several yards behind the center. His hands are outstretched. He places one knee, the one closest to the kicker, on the ground. The other foot is stretched toward the center.

The center snaps the ball back to the ball-holder who places it upon the marked spot with one end down. He holds the top of the ball in place with one or two fingers.

Making the Place Kick. If you are the kicker, stand one or two steps behind the ball. Spread your feet a few inches apart, with your knees slightly bent and your hands hanging loosely at your sides or resting upon your knees. Let your body lean slightly forward with your kicking toe pointing straight ahead. To make the kick—

1. Take your hands off your knees.
2. Take one step forward with your kicking foot.
3. Take a second step forward with the opposite foot, landing just to the side of the ball.
4. Keeping the knee of your kicking leg bent and stiff, kick the ball just below the middle point.
5. Follow through by raising your kicking leg high. Keep the weight on your other toe. Bend your body forward to avoid falling backward.

"Field-goal" Kick. The "field-goal" kick can be made from any place on the field and at any time during a game. This kick can be long or short. It is made in the same way as the place kick.

Punting Drills

1. Take your "punting stance" and walk through the kicking motion with or without a ball.
2. Mark a spot on the field. See which player can punt the ball closest to that spot.
3. Mark several lines on a field, about ten yards apart. See which player can punt the ball to the farthest line.

Punting Goal Game

The idea of this game is to punt the ball as far as possible into the opposite team's territory. This game helps improve accuracy and gain distance in kicking. It also gives you practice in catching punted balls.

Mark a goal line at each end of the field. Mark another line at the center of the field. One team starts the game by punting the ball from the center of the field into the opposite team's territory.

The receiving team punts the ball back from the spot where it was caught. If the ball is kicked over the enemy goal line on a fly, the kicking team receives three points. If the ball just rolls over the line, it's worth one point.

If a player catches a punted ball "on the fly," he

takes three long running steps forward from the spot of the catch and punts the ball back toward the other team's line. A ball not caught on the fly is punted from the spot where the player touched it or where the ball stopped. Change goals after each score. This game can be played by two or many players.

CHAPTER **6**

HOW TO CATCH PASSES, PUNTS, AND KICKS

It's a thrill to make a nice catch for a long gain or touchdown. But a football, because of its odd shape, is often as hard to catch as a greased pig. If you find it hard to hold on to the ball, don't be discouraged. Start with simple catches and keep on practicing. Soon you will find that you can control the ball.

Stationary-pass Catch—*Waist-high*

1. Take a short run to about 6 to 10 yards away from the passer.
2. Stop, turn and face the passer. Keep your elbows bent loosely against the side of your body.
3. Bend forward just a little and form a "cup" with your hands. To form a cup, the palms of both hands face the passer with the fingers spread and

PASS-RECEIVING

WAIST-HIGH

ABOVE-THE-WAIST

with the little fingers of both hands touching.

4. As the ball reaches your hands, trap it by bringing it against your body.
5. Control the ball and run.

Above the Waist. This is often called the "face pass."

1. Raise your hands to the same height as the pass, with your palms facing the passer, and the thumbs of both hands touching.
2. After the ball falls into this "cup," quickly trap it by bringing it down to your waist.
3. Control the ball and run toward the goal.

"Over-the-Shoulder" Catch. *On the run.*

1. Run out for a pass.
2. If the pass is coming on your right side, turn your head and look over the right shoulder. Stretch both arms forward and upward with your palms facing the passer and your little fingers touching.
3. Make the catch by letting the ball drop into this "cup."
4. Hug the ball and run down the field for a touch-down.

When you can make a catch like this, you're really getting there.

PASS·RECEIVING HINTS

Keep your fingers, hands, and arms loose when making a catch.

As you catch the ball, trap it against your body.

Pass-receiving Drills. *For one player: without a ball.*

1. Practice the waist-high, above-the-waist, and over-the-shoulder catches.
2. Try these same drills with a ball and a partner.
3. For one player with a ball:

   Toss a ball upward, toward the right, the left, the front, the back, and forward.

See how well you can catch the ball from every direction.

OVER·THE·SHOULDER PASS·RECEIVER

Two-player Drills

1. Stand about 3 yards apart, facing each other. One boy acts as the passer and the other is the receiver. Try the waist-high, below-the-waist, and above-the-waist passes. As you improve, increase the throwing distance.
2. The passer will toss the ball toward the right. Then toward the left. Catch these passes.
3. Now try catching these passes "on the run." Make your catches on a slow run and gradually increase your running speed when you can make these catches well.
4. Arrange with the passer where he will throw the ball. Make a "zigzag" run down the field and catch the ball. In a game, this kind of play fools the opposing players. Are you beginning to see some improvement in the way you handle the ball?

Catching Punts and Kicks

Kick-receiver's Duties. Anyone on a team may receive or "catch" a kick. The player who stands farthest back on the field to catch most of the opponents' punts and kicks is called a "safety man." He must be a good punt receiver. A good receiver must know:

1. How to catch punts and kickoffs from a standing position, and on the run.

2. When to make a "fair catch." A fair catch is made when the receiver is surrounded by many enemy players and does not want to take a chance of perhaps fumbling the ball on the catch.

In a case like this, the receiver gives a signal by raising his arm up high before catching the ball. This signal means, "Hands off, everybody! The ball is mine." Now the receiver cannot be tackled by enemy players. But if he fumbles the ball, it becomes a "free ball" and anyone may try to get it. After a fair catch, your team takes possession of the ball at that spot for the next play.

3. When it is better not to touch a kicked ball. Do not touch a kicked ball if you see that it will be hard to handle. A ball is hard to handle when it is too close to the ground, bouncing in all directions, or

FAIR CATCH

when there are too many enemy players nearby.

Catching Punts "on the Fly." The ball is in the air. Get ready to catch it.

1. Stand far enough away so that you will have to run toward the ball.

2. Try to judge the distance the ball will travel.

3. Run swiftly in line with the flight of the ball and get directly under it.

4. Form your pocket and wait for the ball.

5. As the ball hits your hands, trap it against your body.

6. Hug the ball under one arm and run.

Catching Punts "on the Bounce." If a punted ball is coming at knee-level or lower, don't try to catch it on the fly.

Run to about 5 to 10 yards behind the spot where

CATCHING BOUNCING PUNT

you think the ball will land. If the ball bounces toward the right or left, you are in position to go after it. Should the ball take a high bounce, run quickly and catch it before it drops.

PUNT-CATCHING HINTS

Always be in position to run up toward the ball.
To prevent fumbling, always pick up the ball with both hands.

Drills for Catching Punts and Kicks

It is not easy to catch punts and kicks. Even the champions had trouble when they started. Let's begin by trying these simple drills.

Catching Punted Ball "on the Fly." *For two players: with a ball.*

CATCHING PUNT ON FLY

1. This drill will give practice in catching and kicking. Two players face each other about 20 yards apart.

   One player will punt to the receiver. Take turns at catching and kicking.

2. A punted ball is rolling on the ground. Pick up the ball with both hands. Hug it and run.

3. *Catching Kickoff Ball. For several players.*

   One player holds the ball for the kickoff. Another player is the kicker. All other players act as ball-receivers.

   After the ball is kicked, the player closest to the ball yells, "I've got it" before he makes the catch.

   All players should take turns as ball-holders, kickers, and receivers.

CHAPTER 7

CARRYING THE BALL

Many years ago a schoolboy in England picked up a ball and ran with it down the field. Today, running is one of the best ways of advancing a football.

The player running with the ball is called a "ball-carrier." The best ball-carriers are not always the fastest runners. The fine ball carrier is wide-awake and able to think quickly.

The Ball-carrier. During a game, one never knows when he may become a ball-carrier. This may take place—

> at the kickoff
> on a punt
> on an intercepted-pass play
> when receiving the ball from center
> when catching a forward pass

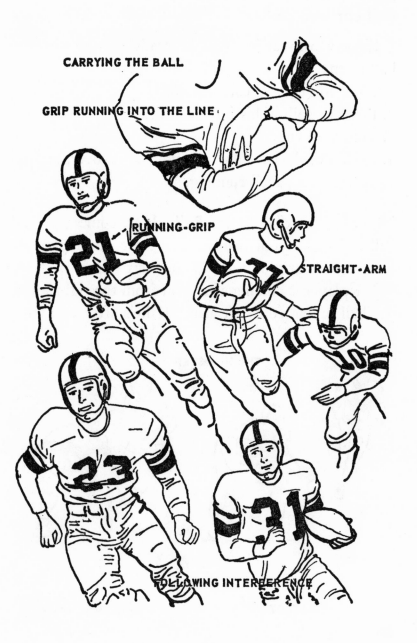

CARRYING THE BALL

GRIP RUNNING INTO THE LINE

RUNNING-GRIP

STRAIGHT-ARM

FOLLOWING INTERFERENCE

Ball-carrier's Duties

Since a ball-carrier must be ready to run with the ball at any time, he must know—

1. How to grip and carry the ball.
2. How to follow his interference.
3. Where to run.
4. How to side-step, dodge, pivot, cross-over, and do "change-of-pace" running.

"Running Back" a Punted Ball. Here comes a punted ball right into your hands. Make the punting catch. Keep a firm grip on the ball and start running.

If a player is coming after you from the right, place the ball under your left arm. If he's after you from

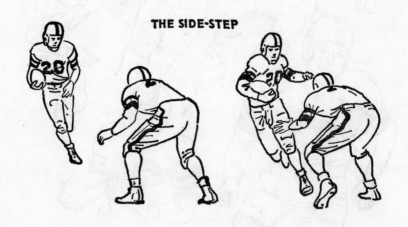

THE SIDE-STEP

READY WEIGHT ON LEFT FOOT

the left, place it under your right arm. When it is necessary to run into a line of players, hold the ball against your body with both hands.

Following Your "Interference." As you run with the ball, some of your teammates run with you or ahead of you to protect you from enemy players. They are known as your "interference." They prevent the opponents who want to stop you. A smart ball-carrier knows how to use his interference to good advantage. This is the way interference works:

1. The center snaps the ball to you.
2. Grip the ball under your right arm, ready for a right-end run.
3. Your interference runs in front to guard you.

RIGHT FOOT SIDE-STEP   **THE DODGE**

4. With short, quick steps, run behind your interference.

5. As soon as your opponents are out of the way, forget your interference and run as fast as possible toward your opponents' goal.

"Change-of-pace" Running. "Change-of-pace" running is knowing when to run fast, when to slow down, or when to streak away. By changing your running speed, you can fool the player who wants to stop you. Before he knows what has happened, streak away for a touchdown.

"Side-Step" and "Dodge" Running. "Side-stepping" and "dodging" will also puzzle your opponent.
Example: You are running with the ball. An opponent is coming at you from your left, ready to stop you:

1. Tuck the ball under your right arm.

2. Just as your opponent is about to reach for you, put all your weight on your left foot, bend that knee a little, extend your left arm for protection and push yourself away from him.

3. With your right foot, take a quick side-step toward the right and speed off.
If the ball is under your left arm, make the side-step with the left foot.

"Cross-over" Step. Champion football players use the "cross-over" step very often during a game.

Example: You are running with the ball held under your left arm. Your opponent is in front of you. Just as he reaches out to stop you:

1. Put all your weight on your left foot.
2. Cross your right leg in front of the left.
3. Extend your right hand for protection and streak away.

The "Pivot." The "pivot" step helps the ball-carrier "roll away" from the tackler. Hold the ball against your body with both hands. As you are about to be stopped by enemy players:

1. Bend your body slightly forward.
2. Pivot, or spin away, from your opponent with short, choppy steps and keep running.

FOOTWORK ON CROSS-OVER

The Running "Straight-arm." The "straight-arm" is also known as the "stiff-arm." It protects the ball-carrier and the ball. It can be used when dodging, when side-stepping, or when pivoting away from a tackler.

Example: You are running with the ball. A player is ready to stop you:

1. Straighten the arm nearest your opponent.
   Keep this outstretched arm between yourself and his shoulder or head.

2. Push yourself away, and step off, and run.

HINTS FOR BALL-CARRIERS

Obey health rules. Also practice skipping rope to keep your legs and body in good condition.

Know how to hold on to the ball.

THE PIVOT

READY FOR SPIN   STEPS FOR TURN

Always carry the ball under the arm that is farthest
away from the tacklers.

Run toward the space where there are the fewest
enemy players.

Always keep some interference between yourself
and your opponents.

Ball-carrier Drills

Cross-over, Side-step, and Pivot Drill

1. Take a short run. Side-step toward the right (or
left) and keep running.
2. Do this same drill with the cross-over step.
3. Practice this drill using the pivot.

Running In and Out between Tires. This drill
teaches balance, accuracy, and high-knee running. If

GETTING AWAY   COMPLETING SPIN   RUNNING

you don't raise your knees, you may fall flat on your face.

Collect six worn-out tires. Place them on the ground in two rows, with three tires in each row and all touching.

1. With a regular "running-grip" on the ball, stand about 5 yards away from the first tire.
2. Start with a slow run and step with your left foot into the first tire on your left.
3. Place your right foot into the first tire on your right. Continue down the line until you have stepped into each tire. If you don't have tires, draw circles on the ground.

Do this exercise a few times. Then increase your speed as you step into the circles.

"Ball Exchanging." *From one hand to the other.* This drill teaches a player to hold on to the ball while running.

1. Hold the ball tightly under your right arm.
2. Run a short distance. Then, shift the ball quickly under your left arm. Do this drill over and over.

Football can be as fast a game as you want to make it. But remember, good teamwork is needed for a successful running game.

CHAPTER 8

HOW TO PLAY QUARTERBACK

Did you know that the quarterback is the most active player on the team? No matter what takes place on the field, he gives the order for the play, and also takes part in the action.

Like a champion chess player, the quarterback follows every move on the field. He plans ahead from the beginning of the game to the very end. He must make many "on-the-spot" decisions, because he has the full responsibility of running the team.

Because it's such an exciting job, all young boys want to be quarterbacks. But don't rush. Try playing the other positions, too. Then, as you grow bigger and stronger, you will be able to choose the position that is best for you.

Qualifications of the Quarterback

What kind of person makes a successful quarterback? He must be alert and think quickly. He should be a good leader, and be liked and respected by his teammates. Above all, he must be able to keep calm when things are not going well.

Duties of the Quarterback

1. He must know all the team signals, and call them loudly enough to be heard.
2. During the huddle, he tells what the next play will be and chooses the player who will carry the ball.
3. He must know when to call the different plays.
4. He tries to find out the strong and weak points of the opposing team as well as his own.
5. He listens to suggestions from his teammates.

Also, he must know how to handle the ball, be a good passer, and know how to tackle, block, and run.

Quite a list of duties, isn't it? Start practicing now. Learn to pass, run, and punt. Play touch football. Little by little, you will learn the game. Then, when you are bigger and stronger, you may try tackling and blocking. Not before!

The Quarterback in Action

In high school and college, the quarterback plays on both offense and defense. Let's watch the school quarterback in action. His team is in a "huddle" talking over the next play. They decide to use the "T-formation."

Out of the Huddle. Here comes the team out of the huddle. The fans wonder what the next play will be. A pass? A run? A "fake" play?

The center is the first to reach the scrimmage line. The rest of the team lines up in the T-formation. The center bends over the ball. The quarterback stands directly behind him. When the T-formation is used, the quarterback is always the first man to receive the ball from the center.

Quarterback's "Stance." 12—77—35! In a loud voice, the quarterback calls the signals. Then he moves up closer to the center player and takes the following stance (left-handers will use the opposite hand and foot):

1. Spread your feet about 12 inches apart. Place your right foot a few inches in back of the left. Bend your knees slightly.
2. Keep your back straight and lean forward a bit over the center's body. Look straight ahead.
3. Move both hands under and close to the center's body and form a pocket for receiving the ball.
   a. Hold your hands at knee level about 8 to 10 inches away from your body.
   b. Place your thumbs close together and

spread your fingers, with the fingers of your right hand pointing downward.

c. The back of your left hand should be touching the center's left thigh.

Receiving the Ball from the Center. With a quick "snapback," the center shoves the ball into your hands. The fingers of your right hand should cover the laces of the ball.

As the ball reaches your hands, get a firm grip on it. With your elbows close to your sides, hold the ball at the middle point and bring it quickly against your body.

QUARTERBACK STANCE

RECEIVING BALL

OVER CENTER

HANDS UNDER CENTER

Now you may take a "forward-pass" grip on the ball, or the grip for a "hand-off" or "fake" play. You are also ready to take the steps that will place you in the right position to—

         a. run with the ball

         b. pass it

         c. hand it to another player

To make any of these plays, the quarterback uses the "step-out" or "spin-out."

The "Step-out"

1. Step off with your right foot and make a quarter-turn to the right.
2. With the left foot, continue this turn until you have made a half-turn and are facing your backfield players.

MAKING THE STEP-OUT

The "Spin-out"

1. Bend your right foot slightly and move it in back of the left foot. Keep most of your weight on your right (back) foot.
2. Spin on the ball of your right foot and make a half-turn toward the right to face your backfield players. Both the step-out and the spin-out can be made either toward the right or left. Use whichever is best for you.

Handing the Ball to Backfield Player. When the ball is handed to a backfield player, it is called a "hand-off" play. It is done like this:
1. Hold the ball with both hands.
2. Move both arms toward your left side.

   Your right halfback is running toward you. When he comes close enough—

1   2

HANDING BALL TO BACKFIELD PLAYER

3. Place the ball between his arms, which are ready to receive it.

   With the ball hugged tightly to his body, the halfback will run toward the open field.

   To make a hand-off to the left halfback, hold the ball out on the right side.

"Faking" Hand-offs. A "faking" play is done to fool the enemy team. The quarterback pretends to hand the ball to a backfield player, but instead, he keeps it and throws a pass, or runs with the ball himself. This play is known as a "fake hand-off."

The "Passing" Quarterback

The Forward Pass. After you (quarterback) receive the ball from the center—

1. Adjust the ball in your hands, making sure that your fingers are over the laces.
2. At the same time, make a quick turn to the right or left.
3. Hurry to a safe position where your teammates are ready to protect you.
4. Turn, so that the side of your body away from your throwing arm faces toward the two teams.
5. With both hands, hold the ball about chest-high. Down the field you see that your "pass-receiver" is free.
6. Raise the ball so that it is level with your ear. Point

the ball toward the teammate who is to catch the pass.

7. With a strong throw, send the ball straight to this player.

The Lateral Pass. After you (quarterback) receive the ball from the center, you are in a crouch position.

1. Remain in this position. Grip the ball with both hands and make a quick quarter-turn in the direction of your "throwing arm."

2. Step off with the foot opposite your "throwing arm," and move toward the player who is to make the catch.

3. With your grip underneath the ball, make an under-

1   **2**

FAKE HAND-OFF TO LATERAL-PASS

3   **4**

hand toss at hip level toward a teammate who is running along on your right side.

This play is often called a "pitch-out" lateral pass.

Quarterback "Strategy"

Working out a football play is very much like doing a problem in arithmetic. You study the problem and then decide upon a way to solve it. In football, working out winning plays is called "strategy."

Field-condition Strategy. Before a game, the quarterback, the captain, and the coach examine the entire playing field. Is the field in good condition? Are there wet spots anywhere?

This information helps the quarterback decide which plays he will use on the different parts of the field.

Wind Strategy. Is it a windy day? If so, is the wind against your team or with it? When the wind is against a team, it is hard for them to throw passes, and punted balls will not travel far. More running plays should be used when the wind is against a team.

With a helping wind, a team can try more punts and passes. Making use of every advantage is smart strategy.

Position of the Ball on Field. A quarterback looks toward the side lines after every play. He checks to see:

1. The number of yards his team must gain for a first down or a touchdown.
2. Whether the ball is lying closer to the right or left side of the field. (Some players run better to their left side than they do to their right.)
3. Whether the team is in position to try for a field goal.

By following the position of the ball on the field, the quarterback decides upon the next play.

Choosing the Plays. When other plays fail, it's wise to call for "punt" plays. Punts are usually called for in these situations:

1. The ball is between your own goal and the 10-yard line. This means that your team is 90 yards away from a touchdown. In this case, the quarterback may call for a punt play on the first down.
2. Should the ball be over the 40-yard line, the punt is usually called for on the fourth down.

Good kicking helps the ball to go farther into enemy territory.

It also saves a team from tiring because of too many running plays.

"Short-gainer" Plays. A quarterback will call for a "short-gainer" play:

1. If a team needs to gain only a few yards to make a first down or a touchdown.
2. To find out if there is a weak spot in the other line.

On short-gainer plays, the quarterback calls for runs straight into the opposing line. These plays are called "straight bucks" or "slants."

"Long-gainer" Plays. A "long-gainer" play is called when:

1. A team is losing.
2. The opposing team is expecting a short-gainer play.
3. The opposing team is "open" and there is a good chance to make long passes and wide end runs.

"Mixing" the Plays. The quarterback mixes his plays to puzzle the other team. He may call for wide end runs, short and long passes, "smashes" through the line, or punts and fancy "spinners." This is smart planning, or strategy.

Using the Right Players. A team usually has a certain player who carries the ball for wide end runs. Another player does most of the passing. Some are best for plunging through the line. Of course, there are those who can do everything well. The wise quarter-back uses the right player at the right time.

It's a thrill to watch a fine quarterback in action. When his team is winning, he keeps everyone "pepped up" so that they will not slow down. If his team is losing, he gives his teammates words of encouragement to keep going.

All fans admire a team that fights to the very end. And this fighting spirit is helped along by the leader-ship of the quarterback.

Quarterback Drills

When the quarterback started out, he played touch football and practiced many drills. Drillwork helps young boys become fine players. Write the drills in your Football Notebook. Then practice until you can do them.

Ball-handling for Quarterbacks

1. Practice receiving the snapback from center in the T-formation play.
2. Drill on the step-out and spin-out.
3. Practice the different hand-offs to your ball-carriers.

Football Quiz Game. *For any number of players.*

When you are at a football game or watching one

over TV, look closely and see what the quarterback did after receiving the ball from the center.

1. Did he take a step-out or spin-out? Did he pass, run, or hand the ball to one of his backfield players?
2. Can you recognize a lateral and a forward pass?
3. What kind of hand-off play was just made? Was it a "fake" hand-off? Was it a quarterback "keep-and-run"?

Mark yourself on this quiz. This game will really sharpen your wits.

Making Charts. Champion quarterbacks make many charts. Usually they make a chart for every play. These charts are often called "strategy maps."

1. On a large sheet of paper, draw a chart of a football field.
2. Put a mark where the quarterback should call for a punt play on—

> the first down
> the second down
> the third down
> the fourth down

3. Place another mark between the yard lines where the quarterback should call for running plays through the line.

87

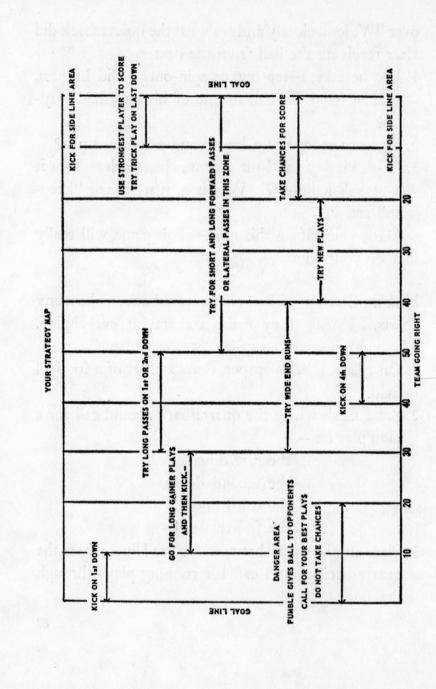

YOUR STRATEGY MAP

GOAL LINE

KICK FOR SIDE LINE AREA

USE STRONGEST PLAYER TO SCORE
TRY TRICK PLAY ON LAST DOWN

TAKE CHANCES FOR SCORE

KICK FOR SIDE LINE AREA

TRY FOR SHORT AND LONG FORWARD PASSES
OR LATERAL PASSES IN THIS ZONE

TRY NEW PLAYS

TRY LONG PASSES ON 1st OR 2nd DOWN

TRY WIDE END RUNS

KICK ON 4th DOWN

TEAM GOING RIGHT

GO FOR LONG GAINER PLAYS
AND THEN KICK.—

KICK ON 1st DOWN

DANGER AREA
FUMBLE GIVES BALL TO OPPONENTS
CALL FOR YOUR BEST PLAYS
DO NOT TAKE CHANCES

GOAL LINE

20   30   40   50   40   30   20   10

4. Put marks on the yard lines where he should call for fancy or wide end runs.

Use different colors for the various plays so that it will be easier to see what is happening on the field. This colorful chart shows how well you can plan winning plays. Study the game and practice it. You, too, may become a champion quarterback.

CHAPTER 9

HOW TO PLAY HALFBACK AND FULLBACK

When you see fancy stepping, smart ball-handling and powerful line plunges, look for the halfbacks and the fullback. These active players use many skills to keep the ball on the move. What makes a good halfback?

The Halfbacks

There are two halfbacks in the backfield, a right and left halfback. Their duties depend upon the team formation. These men play on the offense as well as the defense. This means that they try to score and also do all they can to prevent the opposing team from scoring.

Halfbacks should be strong runners and skilful ball-handlers. They must know how to side-step, dodge, and spin away from enemy players. In fact, the half-backs should be the fastest runners on the field.

Duties of the Halfbacks

A valuable halfback should know:

1. The team plays, the signals, and who will carry the ball.
2. How to run interference.
3. How to pass and catch.
4. How to punt.
5. How to receive punted balls.
6. How to carry the ball.
7. How to block passes.
8. How to tackle.

HALFBACK STANCES

TWO-POINT STANCE   FOR SNAPBACK FROM CENTER

Halfback "Stance."   There are several "stances," but the "two-point stance" shown on page 91 is best for young players.   Many champions use it, too.

"Two-point" Stance.   Feet about shoulder-width apart.   Knees slightly bent.   Hands resting just above the knees.   Keep the head up and look straight ahead.

The Halfbacks in Action.   Your team decides to use the T-formation.   The players come out of the huddle and take their places on the field.   The center leans over the ball.   The linemen get into position on the scrimmage line.   The quarterback stands behind the center.

Position of the Halfbacks.   The right halfback stands about 4 yards behind the right tackle.   The left half-back stands the same distance behind the left tackle and they take their stance.

1 | 2   FAKE HAND-OFF

Receiving the "Hand-off." The center "snaps" the ball to the quarterback. The quarterback spins around and faces his backfield players. He "fakes" a hand-off to the left halfback who runs into the left side of the line. The right halfback begins to run forward with short, choppy steps. Watch him get ready to receive the hand-off.

He raises his left arm with the palm facing the ground and forms an angle in front of his chest. His right hand is in front of his right hip, with the fingers spread and palm facing upward. He is ready to receive the ball.

Very smoothly, he runs into the ball which is in the quarterback's hand, traps it with both hands, and runs down the field. The left halfback may receive a hand-off in the same way on his side of the field.

Halfback Receives the Ball from Center. Whenever a team does not use the T-formation, the halfbacks

AND RUN   3   4

should be ready to receive the "snapback" from center.

Take the two-point stance. Here comes the ball right toward you about hip-high. Get set to receive it.

1. Remove your hands from your knees and keep your elbows close to your body.

2. Spread your fingers with the palms facing upward and form a cup to receive the ball.

3. Trap the ball with both hands, and hug it against your body.

You are ready to get into position to make a pass, quick run, hand-off, or fake hand-off play. Practice these skills which all halfbacks should know.

The Fullback

Did you know that the fullback is one of the most powerful players in the backfield? He is often depended upon to run through the line. He should be able to receive a quick hand-off without fumbling, and

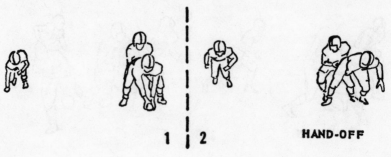

1 2   HAND-OFF

know how to fake a hand-off to another backfield player.

Duties of the Fullback

1. He blocks enemy players who are in front of his team's ball-carriers.
2. He usually helps back up the line players on defensive plays.
3. He runs interference.
4. He is ready to make most of the line "plunges."

Position of the Fullback. The position of the fullback depends upon the play to be made. In the T-formation he stands about 4 yards behind the quarterback and between both halfbacks. The fullback uses the two-point stance or three-point stance.

He receives the direct snapback from center and the hand-off from the quarterback in the same way as the halfback.

TO RIGHT HALF BACK   3 | 4

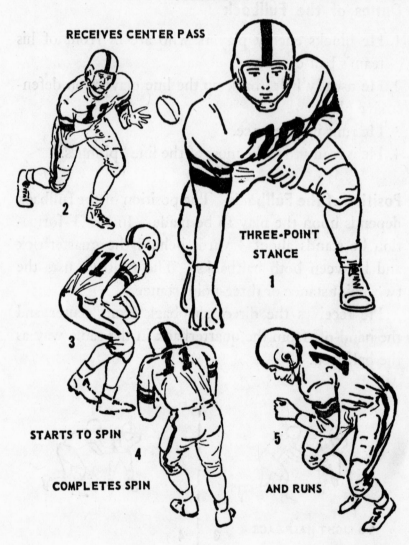

FULLBACK

RECEIVES CENTER PASS

2

**THREE-POINT
STANCE**

1

3

STARTS TO SPIN

4

COMPLETES SPIN

5

AND RUNS

During a game the two halfbacks and the fullback see plenty of action. For good fun and excitement learn to play these positions.

HALFBACK AND FULLBACK HINTS

Know the team signals.

As you take your stance, don't make any unnecessary movements which might let the other team know who will carry the ball.

Control the ball before you run.

Begin your run with short, choppy steps.

Always take advantage of your interference.

Halfback and Fullback Drills

There is a saying, "A child learns to crawl before he can walk." So if a drill seems hard, take it apart, and learn one step at a time.

Practice Drills. *Without a ball.*

1. Practice your stance.
2. Practice running with an imaginary ball.
3. Practice receiving the hand-off with an imaginary ball.

"Hand-off" Drill. *For two or more players.*

Two players face one another about 5 yards apart. One player holds the ball with both hands, about waist-high.

His teammate takes a backfield stance. On the word "Go," the player with the ball takes a short step forward with the left foot and makes a hand-off toward his teammate on his right who is running to receive the ball. Each player takes turns receiving and making the hand-off.

Receiving Center's "Snapback" Ball. *For two or more players.*

This play is made when the team is not using a T-formation. The center leans over the ball ready to make the "snapback."

1. Take the two-point stance about 4 yards in back of the center.
2. Start calling signals.
3. On the word "Go," the center will snap the ball to you about hip-high.
4. Make the catch.

Change places with the center so that he may try this play. Are these drills beginning to go more smoothly? Nice going!

CHAPTER **10**

PLAYING THE LINE

Watch that "forward wall!" See how they keep those enemy runners from gaining ground. They go after opposing ball-carriers. They block and punt enemy passes. They pave the way for their own backfield players. This is modern football as it is played by the seven linemen who make up the "forward wall."

The Ends

You can easily spot the two ends because usually they are the tallest players on the team. Of course there are fine ends who are not so tall but have other skills that make up for their lack of height.

Qualifications of Ends

An end player must—
1. Have a good pair of hands.

2. Have speed in his movements.

3. Like close action.

4. Be a good actor.

5. Know how to carry the ball.

Duties of Ends

Ends keep busy every minute of a game, whether they are playing on offense or defense.

On Defense

1. Ends act as tacklers.

2. They block punted balls.

3. They block passes.

On Offense

1. Ends block opposing players.

2. They catch passes.

3. They are first to go after punted balls.

4. They are always ready to carry the ball.

End Stance. Their stance depends upon the team formation and whether their team is on offense or defense. There are several stances but the "three-point" stance is best at this time.

"Three-point" Stance. This stance is used both for offense and defense.

1. Take your place in the line.

2. Spread your feet a little less than shoulder-width

CATCHING WAIST HIGH PASS

ENDS

CATCHING OVER THE SHOULDER PASS

apart, with the left foot a few inches ahead of the right.

3. Bend your knees and place the knuckles of your right hand lightly on the ground, keeping the arm straight.

4. Rest your left hand slightly above your left knee. Most of your weight should be on the balls of your feet and not on the right hand.

Keep your back straight with your head and eyes up. You are now in a half-crouch position very much like a sprinter who is ready to "take off."

"Getting Free" to Catch Passes

There are many ways of "getting free" to catch passes. They depend upon the play that is being planned or the kind of defense your opponents are using.

"Down-and-out" Run and Catch. As the center snaps the ball to the passer, run straight down the field about 10 yards. Suddenly change direction, run toward the sideline, and catch the ball which the passer throws to you.

To make the "Down-and-in" run and catch, run straight down the field. Change directions and cut inward toward the center of the field to catch the pass.

"Buttonhook" Run and Catch. Run straight ahead. Let your opponent think you are going to run past him. This will make him move back. Stop quickly just before you reach him. Make a little half-circle turn that looks like a "buttonhook." Face your passer and wait for the catch.

There are many other runs to catch passes. You may run outward, then inward, and make the catch. You may also run inward, toward the center of the field, then outward, and make the catch. Make up your own "zigzag" runs.

The Center

Every play starts with the center. The success of every play depends upon the smoothness of the "snapback." But snapping the ball is not all that a center does.

Duties of the Center

1. He must know all the team signals and plays.
2. He must know the various kinds of snapbacks for the different backfield formations.
3. He must snap the ball back with control and accuracy.
4. When his team has the ball he must do blocking after the ball is snapped.

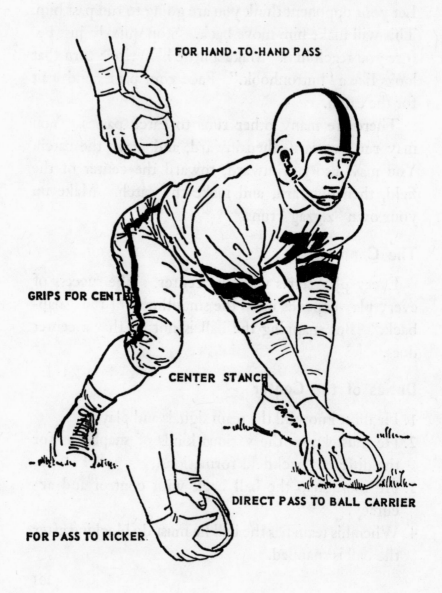

FOR HAND-TO-HAND PASS

GRIPS FOR CENTER

CENTER STANCE

FOR PASS TO KICKER

DIRECT PASS TO BALL CARRIER

5. When his team does not have the ball—
   a. he may be asked to call the defensive plays
   b. he must be ready to tackle as a "linebacker"

Center's "Stance."   Here is one of several good center "stances":

1. Spread your feet a little more than shoulder-width apart with the kicking foot a few inches ahead of the other.
2. Bend your knees and place both hands over the ball. Your arms should be straight.   Do not lean over the ball.   Keep your head even with the back end of the ball.   Keep your back straight.
3. If your team is using the T-formation, look straight ahead.
4. If your team is not using the T-formation, lower your head so that you can see the legs of the backfield player who is to catch the snapback.

Center's "Grip."   The ball is on the ground with the laces facing toward the right.   For left-handers the laces will face left.

1. Place the throwing hand toward the front and a bit under the ball.
2. With the other hand, grasp the middle part of the ball, placing your thumb on top and fingers at the side.   Do not put any weight on the ball.   Your

front hand is ready to do the passing and the other hand will guide the ball.

Center "Passes."   A center must know how to make a number of passes.

1. *"T-Formation" Center Pass.*   This is known as a "hand-to-hand" pass because the center really *hands* the ball to the quarterback.

   a. Take the stance.

   b. Grip the ball.

   c. Lift the ball and move it back into the quarterback's hands.

   d. Release the rear hand.

   e. As you feel the quarterback taking the ball, release the front hand and charge forward.

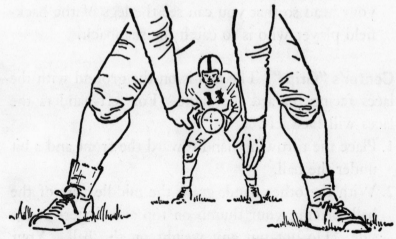

DIRECT PASS TO RUNNING BACK   OR PUNTER

2. *"Direct" Pass to Ball-Carrier.* This pass is used when the team is not in a T-formation.

   a. On this snapback, the center lowers his head so that he can see the receiver's legs.

   b. The receiver stands about 4 yards behind the center.

   c. The center snaps the ball with a smooth motion toward the receiver's waist.

3. *"Long-punt" Pass.* The center places the throwing hand well under the ball. This grip gives the ball more of a lift and carries it a longer distance. This is the longest snapback a center has to make. The player who intends to make the punt receives this pass.

Guards and Tackles

Have you ever wondered why some teams are able to smash through the enemy lines for victories? Why is it impossible to score against certain teams? The answer is, hard-charging guards and tackles. Many top backfield players have said, "Give us good linemen and we will play championship football."

Qualifications of Guards and Tackles

They are the strongest and heaviest players. They like plenty of close action. Many guards and tackles are fine kickoff men and field-goal kickers, too.

Duties of Guards and Tackles

Guards and tackles should:

1. Stop enemy runners from gaining ground.
2. Open up holes in the enemy line to allow their own ball-carriers to run through.
3. Be ready to act as linebackers when on defense.
4. Report the weak and strong points of the opposing team to the quarterback.
5. Know all the team signals and plays.

Stance for Guards and Tackles. The stance depends upon the formation and whether the team is on offense or defense. Guards and tackles may take the regular "three-point" stance but in more of a crouch position.

GUARD AND TACKLE STANCE

To get the crouch position, take a deeper knee-bend so that your hips will be a little lower than your shoulders.

Drills

All linemen should practice the stance and quick "take-offs." Ends should drill on running and catching. A center spends much time trying the different kinds of snapbacks.

End Drills

1. Practice the stance.
2. Do the "Down-and-out" run and catch, with a teammate.
3. Drill on the "Down-and-in" and "Buttonhook" run and catch.
4. Try the "Out-and-in" and "In-and-out" run and catch.

Center Drills

1. Practice the T-formation snapback to a teammate who is acting as quarterback. Take turns making the snapback and receiving the ball.
2. Pin a target upon the side of a barn about waist-high, or hang up an old carpet in a safe place. Stand 4 yards away and aim "center" passes at this target. As your aim improves, increase the distance. After each pass, charge forward.

Drills for Guards and Tackles

1. "Blocking" drill. *For one player without a ball.* Pretend that your team has the ball. Imagine that your center has snapped the ball to a backfield player.

   a. Take your stance.

   b. Start forward with short steps. Place both hands in front of your chest and keep the elbows chest-high.

   c. Try to stop your imaginary opponent by placing your shoulder against his chest and pushing him backward. Keep your feet on the ground all through this blocking drill.

2. "Offense" and "Defense" Team Drill. *For a group of three players.* Two players take their stances side by side, about a yard apart. An opposing player takes his stance facing them, about a yard away.

   On the word "Go," this player tries to get through the line between the two players who will try to "block" him.

Many groups of three may practice this drill at the same time.

"Playing the line," is filled with action and excitement. Study and practice the different positions in the line. You will see the importance of the "forward wall."

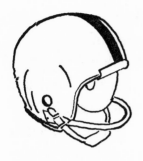

CHAPTER 11

EQUIPMENT

It's fun to play football. You can play on a play-ground, an open field, or a vacant lot. All you need is a football and a pair of gym shoes. And wear your old clothes.

But big league players need a great deal of equip-ment because they play "tackle" football. This equip-ment is their protection against getting hurt. The articles which the players wear are called "personal" equipment. The supplies upon the football field are known as "field" equipment.

"Personal" Equipment

Uniforms belong to the school or football club. Each player has one full uniform which consists of:

a helmet	a pair of football pants
shoulder-pads	a pair of shoes

hip-pads	socks
kneepads	warm-up jacket
thigh-guards	two jerseys, each of
	a different color

Jerseys. A large-sized number is on the front and back of the jersey. Each team wears different-colored jerseys so that the players and fans will not become confused.

Helmet. Every player who takes part in tackle football must wear a helmet. Some helmets have a face-guard fastened to the front in order to protect the face.

Protective "Pads." Players wear kneepads, thigh-guards, and hip-pads under their football pants. Shoulder-pads are worn underneath the jerseys. All this padding helps protect the players.

Shoes. Players wear two types of football shoes. Both are made of very strong leather. There are rubber, plastic, or aluminum "cleats" on the soles.

Line players wear shoes that lace above the ankles. Backfield men and ends wear low-cut shoes because they can run faster in them. But, all players must have their ankles well taped. The place-kicker or field-goal kicker wears a square-toed shoe on the kicking foot.

Other Equipment

Practice "Dummies." Big-league players drill on blocking and tackling with practice "dummies."

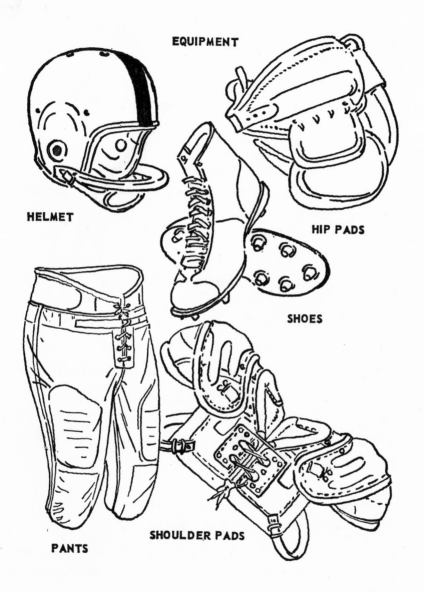

EQUIPMENT

HELMET

HIP PADS

SHOES

PANTS

SHOULDER PADS

These are covered with canvas and stuffed with soft material.

"Driving Sled." A "driving sled" is used for making the leg muscles stronger. Also, it gives players practice in keeping the body low.

Several players place their shoulders against this padded sled and try to push it.

Football "Tee." Before the kickoff, the ball is placed upon a football "tee." This "tee" is made of hard rubber and holds the ball in the right position for the kickoff.

Judging by all this equipment, football is a rugged game. So don't hurry to play tackle. For the time being, enjoy the game of touch football.

Officials' Equipment

At ordinary games, two or three officials are enough. But for important games, seven officials take charge. They are a referee, an umpire, a head linesman, three assistant linesmen, and a field judge. Each one wears a black-and-white striped shirt, a white cap, knickers, black socks, and football shoes.

Referee. The referee has full control of the game. He wears a whistle around his neck, which he uses at the kickoff, to start the play after time-outs, and to indicate when the ball is dead. He also carries a rulebook with which to settle arguments, if necessary.

The referee takes his position behind the offensive team and calls all the fouls that take place behind the offensive team area.

Umpire. The umpire takes his position behind the defensive team. He wears a small horn on his wrist or around his neck. With this horn he signals to the referee when a foul is committed. He calls all the fouls that take place behind the defensive team area.

Linesmen. The head linesman takes his position on one side of the scrimmage line. He carries a pocket-sized football indicator on which he keeps a record that tells what down it is, the number of time-outs taken for each team, and which team kicked off first. He also carries a horn to call fouls that take place at the scrimmage line.

The referee, umpire, and head linesman carry cloths which they drop where a foul is made.

Two assistant linesmen wait on the sidelines with the "chain-marker." They measure to see if a team has made its first down.

A third assistant holds the "down-marker" near the side lines and even with the ball. This is often called the "down-box." This box is fastened to a 4-foot pole. On each side of the box are the numbers 1, 2,

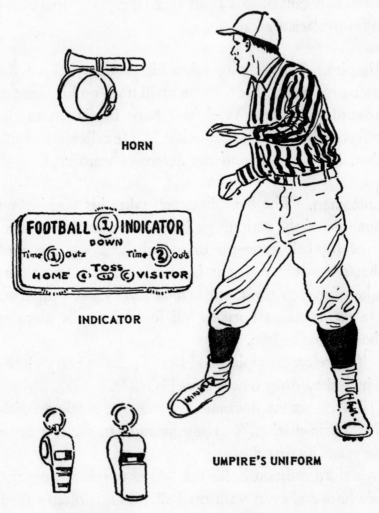

HORN

INDICATOR

UMPIRE'S UNIFORM

WHISTLE

3, and 4. Some "down" indicators are made of four large "flapcards" with numbers on them.

Field Judge. A field judge has a stop watch and a whistle. He takes his place opposite the head linesman. He keeps accurate time of the game. He blows his whistle at the end of each quarter. He "stops" the time when the ball goes off the playing field, checks the time-outs, and all other plays that have time limits. The field judge works closely with the referee.

Field Equipment

A football field is a rectangle and is marked with white lines. A regular football field is 300 feet long and 160 feet wide. An extra 30 feet, which are known as the "end zone," are added to each end of the field.

In high school and college football, the goal posts are located on the end line. In professional football, they are on the goal line.

Lines are marked every 5 yards across the width of the field. This makes the field look like a giant step ladder.

Starting on the 50-yard line, which is at the middle of the field, the "cross lines" are numbered every 10 yards. These numbers read, 50, 40, 30, 20, and 10, on each side of the field. Inside of each sideline and running parallel to them are the "in-bounds" lines. They run the length of the field.

Goal Posts. The goal posts are 18 feet 6 inches apart and stand 20 feet high. Ten feet above the ground a "cross-bar" is fastened to both goal posts. Cross-bars are made of wood, aluminum or steel pipe.

Goal-Line "Corner" Flags. At each corner of the goal line, a flag is set into the ground on a rubber pole about two feet high, which bends easily when a player runs into it.

These flags help game officials decide whether or

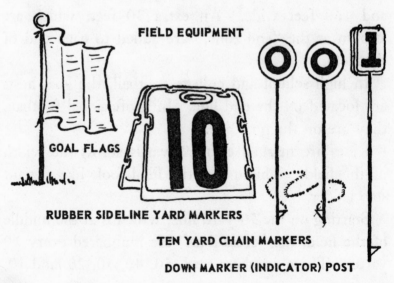

FIELD EQUIPMENT

GOAL FLAGS

RUBBER SIDELINE YARD MARKERS

TEN YARD CHAIN MARKERS

DOWN MARKER (INDICATOR) POST

not a ball carrier stepped over the side lines before crossing the goal line.

"Yardage Chain." The "yardage chain" shows the players how far they must carry the ball to make their first down. The chain is 10 feet long and is attached to the bottom of two rods.

At the beginning of every first down, one end of the chain is placed in line with the ball. The other end is stretched the full 10 yards in the direction of the goal. Every time a team makes a first down, the yardage chain is moved.

Players' Bench. There is a players' bench on each side of the field. These are near the 50-yard line and inside the coaching-box area. Upon these benches you see the players wrapped in blankets on a cold day. When teams play in baseball parks they use the "dug-outs" as benches.

Coaching Box. The coaching box is 40 yards long and 3 yards wide. This box is located 2 yards away from the side lines. The coach walks up and down in the box, near the side lines, following the plays.

Scoreboard. Two big scoreboards are at each end of the playing field where everyone may see them. They tell the score, the downs, how many yards to go for a first down, how much time left to play, and which quarter the game is in. A man operates these score-boards, which are usually run by electricity.

Loudspeakers. There are usually several loudspeakers located at different areas of the football field so that all the fans may hear the announcer. Before the game, the announcer gives the starting line-up for each team. After the kickoff, he gives the names of the player carrying the ball, making the tackle, and making a block. He tells the fans the names of new players entering the game, and their playing positions. In fact, he gives information all through the game.

50-yard-line Seats. All fans would like seats near the 50-yard line. They feel that these are the choicest seats because they give a clear view of the whole field. Of course, everyone can't have a seat near the 50-yard line.

So whether you have one of these prize seats or must watch the game from behind the end zone, you can still have fun at the game and cheer for your team.

CHAPTER 12

GETTING READY FOR
THE BIG GAME

The big day is here! Your team is ready to play touch football against another team. But do you know the many things that must be attended to before you can play this game?

Where are you going to play? Do you have the necessary equipment? Do you have a team captain? Scorekeeper? Referee?

In order to play football, you must be healthy and strong. Champions keep in training and so should you. The training rules are:

Get a proper amount of sleep.

Get plenty of fresh air and exercise.

Eat good nourishing food.

Keep your body clean.

Take care of cuts and bruises.

If you don't feel well, report this at once to your parents or guardian or teacher.

Choosing a Field

If a regular football field is available, use it. Otherwise find a playground, open field, or vacant lot. Be sure to get permission to use the area. Choose a safe place upon which to play. It should be:

far enough away from traffic

far enough away from houses

a dry place

a place that is clear of stones, glass or other dangerous objects

How to Make Your Own Field

After finding a suitable place, look over every inch of ground. Remove tin cans, glass, and high weeds. Roll big rocks away so they will not harm anyone. Place all trash in a box and carry it away. Or dig a deep hole and bury it. Make the ground as level as possible. Then mark the field.

Marking the Field. The playing lines should be marked with chalk or lime. Hardware stores sell regular marking material. Or draw lines into the ground with a stick. Another way to mark the field is to use cloth or cardboard. Put a piece of white cloth or cardboard at each corner of the field and at places where the yard lines connect with the sidelines. Mark the following lines:

1. the goal lines
2. end (zone) lines
3. end zone area

> The end zone area is marked with diagonal or criss-cross lines.

4. the side lines
5. the yard lines

> These lines are drawn every 10 yards across the width of the field from one side line to the other.

6. a spot on each side of the field for the try-for-extra-point after touchdown
7. coaching boxes

Measurements for a "Junior" Touch-football Field

There is no official rule that tells the size of a touch-football field, but here is one that is used by many young players.

1. The field is 60 yards long from one goal line to the other.
2. It is 40 yards wide.
3. An extra 10 yards is added to each goal line for the end zone.

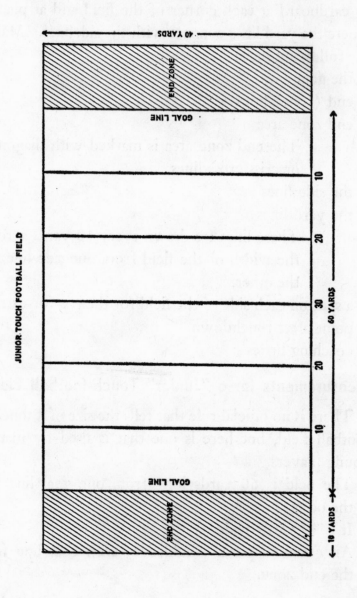

JUNIOR TOUCH FOOTBALL FIELD

Coaching Boxes

There are two coaching boxes, one on each side of the field. They are located 2 yards or more away from the side lines. Each one is 40 yards long. They measure from one 10-yard line to the other. This space is the coaching-box area.

Players' Benches

There are two players' benches, one for each team. Each one is inside the coaching-box area. The benches should be about 5 yards away from the sidelines. They can be made of scrap lumber.

The Scoreboard

Use old boards to make a scoreboard. Set it up where the players and fans can see it. The scoreboard should show:

the names of both teams

the scores made in each quarter

Example:

	1	2	3	4	Total
Lions	0	0	7	7	14
Tigers	6	7	0	7	20

Young Players' "Personal" Equipment

Uniforms. Never allow a lack of equipment to keep you from playing. All you need for touch football are old clothes, a pair of gym shoes and a junior-sized football. But young players may wear the same kind of uniforms as the All-Americans. Uniforms come in all sizes. Team emblems and lettering may be stitched on uniforms by special order.

Shoes. Wear gym shoes with rubber cleats. Big-league shoes are not for you at this time.

Helmet. If you wish, you may wear a helmet. This helmet should fit snugly on your head.

Jersey, Padded Pants, Socks. These articles should all be junior-sized, as this equipment should fit right. A poorly fitted uniform will hinder your movements and slow down your game.

Football. A junior-sized football is 19 inches around the width and 27 inches around the length.

How to Get Uniforms and Equipment

Of course it's nice to play in a full uniform and have all the equipment. But these things are expensive and many young boys cannot afford to buy them. However, you can earn money to buy this equipment. Players can earn money by working together as a team or each one can work for himself.

Working as a Team

1. Help your neighborhood with a "clean-up" drive. Clean yards, mend and paint broken fences, cut grass and water lawns.

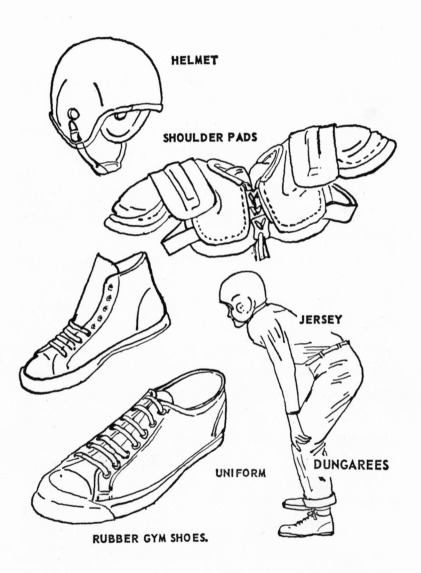

HELMET

SHOULDER PADS

JERSEY

UNIFORM

DUNGAREES

RUBBER GYM SHOES.

2. Collect paper and magazines and sell them to paper-dealers.
3. Organize a delivery service for supermarkets, drug-stores, or other stores in the community.
4. Give a play, puppet show or magic show.

Keep your eyes open for opportunities to help others, and at the same time, help yourselves.

Working Alone

There are many jobs for young boys. You can deliver papers, run errands and take care of lawns. You can shine shoes, make toys, birdhouses, fish flies, and ash trays.

Learn to make attractive and useful things in the neighborhood parks, YMCA's, and settlement houses. Join a class in arts and crafts and sell what you make.

Boys who live in the country can earn money by pulling weeds, picking berries and vegetables, and crating them. You can gather and candle eggs, tend and feed the farm animals, herd sheep or cattle, and clean barns.

Give help where it is needed. But don't try to do anything that is too hard or that you cannot do. Above all, don't do anything without the permission of your parents or guardian.

It may take a long time to earn the whole uniform, so get one article at a time. Some day you will be proud to run out on the field wearing a full uniform that you have worked for and earned.

Game Officials

Captain. Each team must have a captain. This boy should know football. He should be liked and respected by the members of his team. If an argument comes up, the captain represents the team. He settles disputes with the referee or the captain of the opposing team.

Coach. For an important game, an older person should act as coach. His duties are:

1. To decide who will play the team positions.
2. To make substitutions.
3. To explain the opposing team's strong and weak points to his players.
4. To see that the team plays the game according to the rules. If there is no coach, the captain takes care of these duties.

Scorekeeper. Each team has their own scorekeeper. All score sheets should be saved for they are the records of the team's work. The score sheet for each team shows:

> names of players and their positions
> names of players scoring touchdowns, field
>   goals, points-after-touchdown and safeties
> scores made in each quarter
> number of first downs made for each team

If a team wants a more complete record, these figures may be added:

> number of passes thrown
> number of passes completed
> number of passes intercepted
> number of yards gained by running
> number of yards gained by passing
> number of yards each team was penalized

Referee. A grownup should act as referee for an important game. This person should know football. He may be your gym teacher, a parent, an older student, or a member of some football club.

A referee must be fair in his decisions. But sometimes game officials do make mistakes. When this happens there is nothing you can do. The referee's word is final.

Keep this fact in mind: a game is not a matter of life and death. It's nice to win but the idea is to play the game and enjoy it.

Arranging for a Game

Making arrangements for a game is a big job. Many details must be attended to well ahead of time. The captain, coach, or a game committee, may make the arrangements in any of several ways:

1. Phone the captain or coach of the other team asking to play against them.

130

2. Write a letter asking for a game.
3. Visit the other captain or coach and plan the details
   of the game.

Make sure that the other team is a fair match for yours. Teams should be matched as to size, weight, playing ability and experience. If you play a team that is heavier and bigger than yours, the game will probably be one-sided. Also, some of your smaller players may get hurt.

The captain, coach, or secretary should keep a written record of the games to be played. This record should show:

1. Where the games will be played.
2. The number of players on each team.
3. The exact rules that will be followed.
4. The length of the game.
5. The officials for the game.
6. The equipment owned by each team.

After all the arrangements are made, give your team as much information as possible about the games they will play.

"Choosing" for Kickoff

Whether there is a full team or just a few players on each side, the captains must decide which team shall have the choice of kickoff or receiving the ball. This choice is made by the toss of a coin or by guessing.

As a coin is tossed into the air, the captains call for "heads" or "tails." The winner of the toss has the choice of making the kickoff or receiving the ball. The loser may choose which goal his team will defend.

Another way to "choose" is for someone to pick up a handful of pebbles from the ground. Each captain tries to guess the number of pebbles. The closest guess wins the choice.

When the "big moment" comes and your team runs out on the field, remember the saying, "United we stand, divided we fall." If you are united and play as a team, it will be a good game, no matter whether you win or lose. Enjoy the game and have fun.

Touch-football Rules

Players, both young and old, enjoy touch football. The rules are the same as for regular football. The only difference is that in touch football—
1. A player must *not* tackle.
2. A player must not block while his feet are off the ground.

Length of Game. There are four "quarters" in the game. Each quarter runs for eight minutes. At the end of the first and third quarters, both teams have two minutes of rest. At the end of the first half, each team has a five-minute rest period.

Number of Players. If you have enough players, use an eleven-man team. If you do not, there are several choices:

Seven-man Team. This team is made up of four backfield players, one center, and two ends.

Six-man Team. This team has three backfield players, one center, and two ends.

Five-man Team. This team has two backfield players, one center, and two ends.

Less than Five Players. This team will have one backfield player, and the rest will play in the line.

Kickoff. In touch football, there are two ways to kick off. The regular kickoff may be used. Or, the kickoff can be made by punting the ball. This play is always made from the 20-yard line. The receiving team should be at least 10 yards away from the spot of the kickoff or punt.

Punting. During scrimmage play, if a punt is going to be made, the team must announce it before the center "snaps" the ball. No one on either team may cross the scrimmage line until the punt has been made. Also, no one is allowed to "rush," or run toward, the kicker. The penalty for crossing the line too soon, or for not kicking as announced, is 5 yards.

How to Make a "Touch" Tackle.
Regular tackling is not allowed. Instead of tackling, a defensive player just touches the ball-carrier.

Before a game, the team announces whether it will use the "one-hand" or the "two-hand" touch. The kind of touch decided upon must be used all through the game.

A defensive player may touch the ball-carrier anywhere between his shoulder and knees. When using the "two-hand" touch, make the touch with both hands at the same time. After making the touch, stop and raise both hands in the air. The next down will begin at that spot.

If a defensive player does anything more than touch

TOUCH TACKLE

the ball-carrier, it is unnecessary roughness and the team receives a 15-yard penalty.

Blocking. "Body" blocks are not allowed in touch football. However, "shoulder" blocking may be used to stop a player. This is done without using the hands or arms.

To make a "shoulder" block, the blocker keeps both hands against his chest. He must be in an upright position. His feet must remain on the ground.

"Fumbled" Ball. When the ball is "fumbled" it becomes a "dead ball" at the spot where it hit the ground. There is no sense in scrambling for a "dead ball," because the same team that had the ball, keeps it.

But if a team fumbles the ball on the fourth down, without making their 10 yards for a first down, the opposing team gets the ball at the spot where the fumble was made.

Substitutes. There is no limit to the number of substitutes that may go into a game. But substitutions may be made only when the ball is "dead."

Passing. Any number of forward passes may be thrown from behind the scrimmage line. But when a play begins with a kick, a punt, or a kickoff, the receiver may not throw a forward pass. After catching a kicked ball, the receiver may run with the ball or throw a lateral pass. Lateral passes may be made at any time and from any place on the field.

Pass Receiving. Every player on the team is allowed to catch passes at any time, whether they are playing on offense or defense. But everyone should not try to catch the same pass. A few players should guard the passer.

Point-after-touchdown. The try for point-after-touchdown is made from the 2-yard line and may be done in two ways:
1. Throw a pass across the goal line to a teammate.
2. Run with the ball over the goal line.

"Time-outs." Each team is allowed two one-minute "time-outs" in every quarter. But officials or captains may take as many time-outs as they wish for examining players who are hurt, or for settling disputed plays.

Additional Rules

1. A player must leave the game if he shows poor sportsmanship.
2. He must leave the game if he makes a tackle with his feet off the ground.

3. A team loses the ball if a player tries a body block with his feet off the ground.

"Flag" Football

If you would like some extra fun, try "Flag" Football. This game is almost the same as touch football.

Every player wears a cloth tucked into the front and back of his belt. This cloth is called a "flag." Instead of touching a ball-carrier, the defensive player tries to steal one of the runner's flags. Every time a flag is stolen, that player is considered tackled. The player who stole the flag stops at once and waves the flag in the air. The next play starts at that spot.

Touch football is a steppingstone to the regular game. So, on nice clear days, get out into the open and have the thrill of kicking that ball down the field, or making a long run for a touchdown. You will always remember the fun and excitement of touch football.

SCORES AND RECORDS

A coach wants to know how well every man on his team can play. Records are kept of everything each man does in every game he plays.

How many completed passes were thrown during the game? How many yards were gained? How many touchdowns were made? All this information and much more is written down. When are these records filled out? Who does this work? How are records figured? Many people take part in the big job of figuring and record keeping.

Official Scorekeeper

An official scorekeeper is hired for all important games. Both teams, or the Conference Commissioner, choose the scorekeeper. The scorekeeper knows the football rules. He understands the work of the players. The scorekeeper sits in the press box. Upon large sheets of paper he fills in and answers many questions about the team and players.

With him in the press box are the newspaper men, radio and TV announcers who also follow the games closely and keep their own scores.

Team Records

The official scorekeeper answers these questions about both teams:

> Whether the team won, lost, or tied
> Number of points made by each team
> Names of players who scored points and how they made the scores
> Number of first downs
> Total number of yards gained by running (rushing)
> Total yards gained by passing
> Number of passes completed
> Number of incompleted passes
> Number of passes intercepted
> Number of punts and their distance
> Number of fumbles made by each team
> Number of fumbles recovered by opponents
> Number of yards each team penalized

Player Records

These are some of the more important questions the scorekeeper fills in for each player:

1. the name and position of every player in the starting line-up
2. name of every substitute who entered the game
3. number of points made by each player
4. number of yards gained by each ball-carrier
5. number of times each player blocked an opponent's punt
6. number of completed passes caught by a player
7. number of intercepted passes caught by a player
8. number of yards each player was penalized

Passing Records

Each passer is graded upon these plays:

1. number of passes he threw
2. how long each pass was
3. number of passes he completed
4. number of yards gained from completed passes
5. number of passes he threw which resulted in touchdowns
6. the percentage of passes he completed
7. number of passes he threw which were intercepted

Team Scorekeeper

Each team also has a scorekeeper of its own. They

not only keep score but watch everything each player did, such as:

Was he a steady player during the game?

Did he know the team signals?

Did he show good teamwork?

Did he use the proper stance?

Did he argue with the officials?

Did he tire easily?

Was he injured during the game?

Each team also has a team manager. After every game the official scorekeeper gives his report to the managers of both teams. He also sends copies of his reports to the Conference Commissioner. This commissioner sends a copy to the office of the National Commissioner where the records are kept as lasting accounts of the games.

Football teams have offices where these records are also kept. Coaches study them to see the weak and strong points of their players. All players are rated on their ability and skill. That's why these records are so important.

Studying the Records

The coach posts these records in the players' dressing room so they may study them. Players may ask for copies to study more carefully. With the help of these records, the coach works to improve his team.

Football "Program"

Before a game, fans usually buy programs. These look like magazines and give a great deal of information. They give the names of players who appear in the starting line-up, their numbers and positions, and a list of substitute players.

STARTING LINE-UP

	Badgers			Beavers	
No.	Name of player	Pos.	No.	Name of player	Pos.
31	Jerry	LE	17	Jim	LE
48	Len	LT	33	Will	LT
38	Allen	LG	51	Sidney	LG
26	Art	C	22	Charles	C
53	Richard	RG	19	Ron	RG
36	Larry	RT	71	Danny	RT
11	Lester	RE	42	Sol	RE
30	Davy	QB	23	Bobby	QB
18	Hal	LH	41	Dennis	LH
28	Herb	RH	37	Eddie	RH
39	Gordon	FB	63	Louis	FB

The program also shows the team records, players' records, ages, weights, heights, and their home towns.

Figuring "Percentage"

The best place to learn how to figure percentage is in school. Percentage helps you figure the team and player standings. Through the percentages shown in the newspapers the fans learn:

the teams' standings in the league

players' passing averages

players' punting averages
ball-carriers' running averages
pass-receivers' averages

"Team" Percentage. To figure the "team" percentage, or "standing," in the league, take the number of games won and divide by the number of games played. These problems are carried out to three places.

Example: The Badgers have played 6 games. They have won 3 games and lost 3. What is the Badgers' percentage, or standing, in the league?

.500   team percentage in the league

6) 3.000

Players' Passing Averages. To figure the percentage of passes completed, the problem is worked a little differently. Take the number of passes completed, divide by the number of passes tried, then move the decimal point two places to the right.

Example: Bobby completed 6 passes out of 9 tries. What was his passing percentage?

.666   To change a decimal to percentage,
9) 6.000   move the decimal point two places
to the right.
Your answer will be: 66.6 is
Bobby's passing average.

Game Results

Your newspaper prints a record of all games played every week during the football season. This record is known as "Game Results" and tells all that happened between the two teams.

GAME RESULTS

	Badgers	Beavers
First downs	12	15
Yards gained: running	105	130
Yards gained: passing	104	166
Passes thrown	28	26
Passes completed	11	17
Passes intercepted	3	3
Number of punts made	8	6
Average distance of punts (yds.)	34	36
Fumbles	3	3
Yards penalized	25	40

TEAM SCORE BY QUARTERS

Badgers	0	7	7	0	14	
Beavers	14	7	7	0	28	Beavers won 28 to 14

HOW SCORES WERE MADE

Beavers: Touchdowns: Bobby (two); one, on a 15-yard pass from Jerry, and another on a 20-yard run. Dennis made one, on a 2-yard plunge. Jerry made one, on a 40-yard run after catching a punt.
Points after touchdown: Lester (two) Richard (two).

Badgers: Touchdowns: Hal (two); one, on a 10-yard run, one, on a 30-yard run.
Points after touchdown: George (two).

Team Standings

The team standings of each conference are also printed in the sports section.

TEAM STANDINGS

North League

	W	L	T	Pct.	Pts.	O.P.
Badgers	9	3	0	.750	265	170
Lions	7	5	0	.583	254	211
Browns	5	6	0	.455	134	176
Redskins	5	6	0	.455	251	230
Eagles	4	8	0	.333	173	230
Steelers	3	8	0	.273	198	272

South League

	W	L	T	Pct.	Pts.	O.P.
Bears	8	4	0	.667	260	205
Giants	8	4	0	.667	251	231
Packers	7	5	0	.583	303	235
Rams	6	6	0	.500	307	278
Colts	5	7	0	.417	203	211
Cards	3	9	0	.250	218	311

YESTERDAY'S RESULTS

Badgers	21;	Lions	13
Browns	34;	Packers	28
Bears	10;	Redskins	3
Giants	27;	Eagles	20
Rams	37;	Steelers	21
Colts	21;	Cards	20

GAMES SATURDAY

Bears at Giants
Lions at Eagles
Rams at Browns
Colts at Steelers
    Only games scheduled

Key to figures:
W   games won
L   games lost
T   games tied
Pct.   percentage of games won by the team
Pts.   total points scored by the team in all the games played
O.P.   the number of points scored by their opponents

145

More Newspaper Records

Still more records show:
>leading ground-gainers
>leading passers
>leading pass-receivers
>leading scorers

Leading Ground-gainers

Player	Team	Atts.	Yds. gnd.	Lngst. gain	Av.
Harvey	Eagles	202	942	69	4.7
Don	Owls	204	700	25	3.4
Chuck	Badgers	167	673	28	4.0
Tony	Beavers	129	621	62	4.8
Len	Rovers	127	616	46	4.9
Bobby	Giants	134	577	56	4.3
Burl	Bears	127	538	67	4.2
Johnny	Lions	154	532	51	3.5
Jerry	Robins	143	529	41	3.7
Ronny	Colts	136	528	41	3.9

These standings are based on the total yards gained by running.

Atts. means the number of times player attempted to carry the ball.

Yds. gnd. means the total number of yards gained by player carrying the ball.

Lngst. gain means the longest gain made by the player carrying the ball.

Av. means the average yards gained from each run.

Leading Passers

Player	Team	Stndg.	Att.	Comp.	T. yds. gained	Tchdwn. passes	Pct. comp.	Intcpt.	Av. yds. gained
Steve	Giants	1	110	63	1229	9	57.3	8	11.17
Burl	Bears	2	167	99	1508	11	59.3	10	9.03
Nick	Colts	3	301	172	2550	24	57.1	17	8.47
Larry	Tigers	4	265	132	2105	20	49.8	21	7.94
Wally	Redskins	5	200	87	1568	10	43.5	15	7.84
Jimmy	Cardinals	6	279	176	2157	13	63.1	15	7.73
Stan	Browns	7	232	128	1712	11	55.2	11	7.38
Danny	Robins	8	185	84	1321	6	45.4	16	7.14
Frank	Lions	9	215	117	1489	8	54.4	10	6.93
Eddie	Stars	10	289	139	1900	11	48.1	12	6.57

These standings are based on the average yards gained for each pass attempted.

Stndg. means the standing of the passer in his conference.

Att. means the number of passes a player threw.

Comp. means the number of passes a player completed.

T. yds. gained means total yards gained from completed passes.

Tchdwn. passes means the number of passes that went for touchdowns.

Pct. comp. means the percentage of passes completed.

Intcpt. means the number of passes that were intercepted.

Av. yds. gained means the average yards gained from each pass.

147

Leading Pass-receivers

Player	Team	Recd.	Yds. gnd.	Lngst. gain	T.D.
Merrill	Colts	52	757	40	6
Joe	Eagles	47	800	67	6
Herb	Gaints	46	630	48	2
Art	Stars	41	588	63	4
Sam	Badgers	40	687	82	7
Dick	Beavers	38	727	77	5
Al	Bears	37	530	32	1
Frank	Lions	37	458	43	2
Tom	Rovers	34	583	38	3
Burt	Browns	33	624	65	5

These standings are based on the total number of passes received by a player.

Recd. means the total number of passes received by a player.

Yds. gnd. means the total number of yards gained from passes received.

Lngst. gain means the longest gain made from a pass received.

T.D. means the number of touchdowns made from passes caught.

Leading Scorers

Player	Team	T.R.	T.P.	T.T.	E.P.	F.G.	Tot. pts.
Bobby	Giants	4	2	6	17	8	77
Morris	Beavers	0	0	0	31	15	76
Harvey	Eagles	2	0	2	26	12	74
Frank	Robins	1	0	1	23	14	71
Tom	Bears	0	0	0	38	11	71
Burt	Lions	4	7	11	0	0	66
Phil	Browns	0	0	0	32	10	62
Dick	Rovers	9	1	10	0	0	60
Henry	Owls	0	0	0	33	0	60
Bill	Badgers	5	4	9	0	0	54
Paul	Cardinals	6	3	9	0	0	54

These standings are based on total number of points scored.

T.R. means total touchdowns scored by a run.

T.P. means total touchdowns scored from a pass.

T.T. means total touchdowns scored by player.

E.P. means number of extra points scored after a touchdown.

F.G. means total number of field goals kicked.

Tot. pts. means total number of points scored by player.

School, playground, and neighborhood teams keep records, too. You can keep records of your team and players in your Football Notebook.

But for the big-league teams, men and women sit at desks all through the football season and work on figures and percentages. And this work results in the scores and records that make up football history.

CHAPTER **14**

IF YOU CAN'T PLAY FOOTBALL

A certain president of the United States wanted to play football when he was in college. He was not big or heavy enough to make the team. Do you know what he did? He became manager of his college team.

Many well-known men could not play football for one reason or another. But this did not stop them from taking part in other ways and enjoying the game.

Before young boys go out for football, they should get permission from their parents. They should also be examined by a doctor. Sometimes, a doctor will forbid a boy to take part in active sports. So, if you can't play football, don't feel sorry for yourself. There are many ways in which you can still take part and enjoy the game.

Read this list of suggestions and decide what you would like to do.

1. Follow the games.
>   Listen to games over the radio or watch on TV.
>
>   If possible, go to football games.
>
>   Read about football in books, magazines, and the newspapers.

2. Help arrange for games.
>   Be a team secretary.
>
>   Keep the team records.

3. Help the business manager.
>   Take charge of the money used by the club.
>
>   Keep a record of club expenses.

4. Help with publicity.
>   Advertise your team.   Make signs and posters to let people know when and where your team will play.

5. Be a newspaper reporter.
>   Report the games for your school newspaper.
>
>   Write up the games for your neighborhood newspaper.

6. Be a scorekeeper.
>   Keep score of the games.
>
>   Write a report of what every player does on the field.   Figure out playing records and percentages.

7. Be a "chain" official.

Carry the chain into the field and measure
the yards gained.

8. Be a cheerleader.

   Make up cheers, yells, and songs.

   Train the other cheerleaders.

9. Help mark the field.

   Markings wear out. Prepare the field before a game. See that the marking is fresh
   and clear.

10. Take care of supplies and equipment.

    Help make field equipment.

    Mend articles that can be repaired.

11. Help the coach.

    Print the forms for new plays. This is done
    on an office machine.

12. Be a coach's assistant.

    Certain players need special drills.

    See that they carry out the coach's instruc-
    tions when they practice.

Perhaps you can even do a little light practicing
yourself. After you decide what you would like to
do, talk it over with your parents. They may wish
to ask the doctor if he thinks you may do what you
have chosen. Show these simple drills to your doctor
and see if he will allow you to practice them.

1. Toss the ball.

   Toss the ball to another player, so that he

may practice catches or runs. It will help him improve his game. In this way, you will help your team.

2. Pass the ball.

Try passing the ball to a player for distance and accuracy. This will give your teammate practice in catching.

3. Act as center.

Make "snapbacks" to ball-carriers who need practice in carrying the ball.

4. Kick the ball.

This will give players the practice they need in catching and running the ball back.

Do *not* run when doing these drills.

WARNING!

Only after you have the permission of your parents, and your doctor, should you make plans to help your team.

If your parents and the doctor decide that these duties and drills are not for you, remember that a great many boys do not play football either. But you can always watch the games and have the fun of rooting for your team. And, it's always exciting to talk football.

CHAPTER 15

GET INTO THE GAME

There's a tang in the air. The days are crisp and cool. Leaves tumble down from the trees. High in the sky, flocks of birds fly to the south. People get ready for the cold months ahead. It's the fall of the year. It's football time.

Upon playgrounds and fields, all over the country, boys and men happily practice football. They throw long and short passes. They run, side-step, and pivot. They punt and kick.

The sports pages are filled with stories about new players and old-time favorites. Who will make All-American this year? Who will win the Conference title?

Men and women, boys and girls, stream into football fields and stadiums. They wear heavy coats and carry blankets. They buy programs. Team officials look over the field.

Stop! The crowd stands. As the American flag flies in the wind, the band plays The Star-Spangled Banner.

Look! The teams run out on the field. Cheerleaders jump and do handsprings as they lead the team yells. Pretty girl majorettes twirl batons and do fancy steps.

Listen! There goes the referee's whistle. It's the kickoff! Go! Team! Go! Get into the game. There goes a new "Speedy Pete." He runs down the field for a touchdown!

Yes. It's football time again. Football—the great field game.

155